$3\frac{50}{}$
C+H

(6 5 , , , / 6)   JUN 20 '88

DIALOGUE IN DESPAIR

DIALOGUE

IN DESPAIR

PASTORAL COMMENTARY
ON THE BOOK OF JOB

WILLIAM E. HULME

ABINGDON PRESS
Nashville
New York

SET UP, PRINTED, AND BOUND BY THE
PARTHENON PRESS, AT NASHVILLE,
TENNESSEE, UNITED STATES OF AMERICA

TO
SALLY, DALE,
POLLY, MARCIA,
AND LANCE

CONTENTS

CONTENTS

I

PASTORAL COUNSELING
IN THE BOOK OF JOB

1. UNIQUE RESOURCE FOR OUR DAY

The Book of Job is recognized primarily for its valuable contribution to whatever answer there is to the universal question of why man must suffer. It is also recognized as a serious investigation into whether one's loyalty to God is dependent upon his being favored by God. Because of these primary contributions and even as a by-product of them, the book is also a biblical resource in pastoral care. It presents the dynamics of suffering and healing within the framework of the pastoral relationship. Unfortunately this pastoral resource has been largely overlooked because of the greater interest in the theological issues involved in Job's suffering.

As Job's soul is bared, the reader perceives the feelings of the sick and afflicted—their frustration and despair—with which he can empathize. This identification with the sufferer is a pastoral response—even though Job's three pastoral counselors failed to give it. Their failure, however, only provoked Job to expose his feelings more strongly, even to exaggerate them in defiance.

9

The pastoral process which we see in the Book of Job is recognized largely by induction since the book contains no actual dialogues. Instead the conversation is presented in poetry and each participant is given his turn to speak. In spite of this literary format the dynamics of the pastoral encounter are remarkably portrayed. The poetic renditions vibrate with the charge and countercharge of a heated exchange.

The interpersonal dynamics in the book are easily perceived in our day of psychological insight. There is always the danger, therefore, that what we perceive is more what we project into the book than what is actually there. In Job, however, the psychological implications are spelled out by the characters themselves. My task is simply to elucidate the pastoral significance of these implications in terms of our contemporary pastoral awareness. In so doing I am utilizing our growing body of knowledge in the pastoral area to see more deeply into the significance of the Word for our day. Consequently we may see more in Job for pastoral care than the original writers. The genius of the book—not to mention its inspiration—is in its content rather than in the conscious intentions of the writers. An artist's creation may communicate beyond his own awareness.

Although the insights into pastoral care in Job exist in our minds prior to our recognizing them in the book, the fact that we perceive them in the book confirms and even enhances these insights. The raw material is in Job, and Job belongs to the pastoral heritage. This is a distinct advantage since it provides a biblical and theological orientation to pastoral counseling which in its recent evolution has been highly indebted to the psychological sciences. We are even obligated to these sciences for our pastoral insight into Job.

Yet this indebtedness is a source of embarrassment. Is the pastoral counselor any more than a psychologist who believes in

God? This embarrassment would be relieved if pastoral counseling—in fact the whole pastoral care movement—had a theological basis. I personally believe that it *has* such a basis and that the psychological insights can be incorporated into this basis rather than existing alongside it. Christian theology is based on the revelation of God as it is recorded in the Bible. Here is actually a book in this Bible that is focused on the function of pastoral care, as the mental suffering of Job, the pastoral procedure for healing, and the results of the healing process are described in the native milieu of the pastor's theological heritage. Job's encounter with his comforters is by its very context a religious encounter. The theological dimension within which their relationship is viewed is natural to the setting. In this ancient document the psychological insights are extracted from the religious context. The motif is obviously theological. Instead of being psychologized, the religious dimensions of the Jobian dialogues form the structure for the psychological descriptions.

2. UNIQUE THERAPY FOR OUR DAY

Our concern over the psychological orientation to pastoral care is culturally conditioned by the division that exists today between the psychiatric and the religious. Job's problems produced an existential conflict. The healing of emotional conflicts was originally a religious or pastoral concern. Today the religious healer is on the periphery—primarily a source of referral for the psychiatrist. Granger Westberg has raised a pertinent question: What if Sigmund Freud had been a rabbi instead of a physician? The medical profession is now responsible for the treatment of suffering that was once the prerogative of the priest.

The discoveries of Freud have been a decided help to the de-

11

velopment of pastoral care. His descriptions of man's internal conflict, his insight into the phenomenon of repression, and his stress on communication for healing have played a significant role in this development. Since Freud himself took a dim view of religion's therapeutic value, his assistance to clergymen is somewhat ironic. It may be also ironic that the current attack on Freud is coming from psychiatrists and psychologists more than from clergymen.

Yet it may not be really so ironic. Freud's emphasis on the relationship of motives to behavior, on catharsis, and on self-understanding are all in line with biblical emphases. A critic of Freud, psychologist O. Hobart Mowrer, chides clergymen for being "taken in" by Freud. What he fails to see is that Freud may be nearer to the angels than Mowrer. He faults Freud for not taking the value system of the human conscience seriously and then goes to the other extreme of absolutizing the conscience. While criticizing Freud for considering guilt as neurotic, he insists that guilt is real. To Mowrer this means that the guilty one must do his own atoning. The result is religion without a Christ.

Mowrer also criticizes Freud for undermining individual responsibility. On this point the clergy can scarcely be charged with Freudian complicity. In the doctrine of original sin the helplessness of the sinner is presented in tension with the responsibility of the sinner. This tension is preserved in pastoral counseling as the necessity for the person who needs help to retain the responsibility for his problem and its resolution. While environmental complications reduce human freedom, they do not eliminate it.

Pastoral counseling is a therapy based on the assumption that man exists not only in relation to himself and his fellows but also before God. The psychiatrist and the psychologist may also share this assumption, but they do so only as individuals and not by virtue of their professions. Pastoral counseling is a healing ministry and like psychiatry and psychology is concerned with mental and emotional health, but unlike psychiatry and psychology is not limited to their attainment. Pastoral counseling is concerned primarily with sanctification. While sanctification is related to emotional and mental health, it is not identical with them. The goal of sanctification is the increasing integration of one's life around Christ and his church. Consequently pastoral counseling is concerned with a specific kind of integration.

The healing emphasis in pastoral counseling is centered in the person-to-person setting rather than in the milieu of the community at worship. It is dialogical in nature rather than liturgical. The Anglican and Episcopal Churches have done more than others in the liturgical or sacramental setting for healing. They have prescribed liturgies for the service of the laying on of hands, and also an order for the anointing of the sick. These liturgical forms reflect a healing ministry in the use of sacramentals rather than a healing ministry in the dynamics of a personal relationship.

In contrast to the extraordinary healing ministry that depends to some extent on a charismatic gift, pastoral counseling is an ordinary ministry of healing. The healing ministry of Oral Roberts, for example, centers in his ability to create an impression—even on strangers. Whatever personal relationship the charismatic healer may establish with the person is of secondary importance to his purpose. In the ordinary pastoral ministry the relationship between healer and person is primary. In fact it is the means for the communication of the Spirit's healing power.

Because it centers in interpersonal dynamics, pastoral counseling may be threatening to both the counselor and the counselee. This aspect is clearly revealed in the Book of Job. The three friends found it intolerable to go with Job into the depth of his despair. But when one has the courage to go with another into the depths of interpersonal sharing, the involvement changes both parties. In making himself known to the pastor, the counselee is helped to know himself. In opening himself to this communication, the pastor is opening himself also to his own being. The involvement brings them both to a sobered confrontation with the enigma of human existence. The Book of Job takes its characters into the tragic depths of this enigma with the reckless abandon of the modern existentialist. When these dynamics are placed within the framework of the pastoral relationship, the result is a functional picture of pastoral care.

II

JOB'S CALAMITIES AND COMFORTERS

Job 1–2

The prose prologue sets up the conditions that predispose Job to the religious problem over which he struggles throughout the poetic bulk of the book. Because of the consecutive tragedies that befall him, Job refuses to suppress the conclusion that God is unjust—that he is not as ethical, as moral, as the creatures he has made. The cry that is repeated throughout Job's sufferings is *why!*

1. IT NEVER RAINS BUT IT POURS

The prologue gives the metaphysical basis for the Jobian dilemma—the supernatural drama that precipitated the drama on earth. This metaphysical basis is presented in the metaphor of the contemporary culture. The sons of God came to present themselves before the Lord, and Satan, the adversary, was among them. The Lord challenged Satan about the unimpeachable character of his servant Job. But Satan was unimpressed. Who would not fear God and turn away from evil if God has blessed

15

him with seven sons, three daughters, seven thousand sheep, three thousand camels, five hundred yoke of oxen, and five hundred she-asses, many servants, and a position of power and prestige among his people? "Does Job fear God for nought?" he asks. "Hast thou not put a hedge about him and his house and all that he has, on every side? Thou hast blessed the work of his hands, and his possessions have increased in the land. But put forth thy hand now, and touch all that he has, and he will curse thee to thy face."

It was a defiant challenge and God accepted it. He gave Satan leave to deprive Job of his blessings so long as he spared Job's life.

Judging from the perspective of the contemporary Western mind, any god who would subject a believer like Job to such degradation and suffering just to satisfy a dare from his adversary is as bad as the adversary. In his book *Answer to Job,*[1] psycho-analyst Carl Gustav Jung says that God has projected his own unconscious doubts onto the adversary where he can accept them into his consciousness and deal with them. In other words, God really does doubt Job's integrity but can only face this doubt if it seems to originate with Satan.

The prologue may also be interpreted as a metaphysical expression of God's confidence in Job. Does God really accept Job for what he is or must he be spared the ordeals that afflict so many others? We know that any parent who is determined to spare his child from the problems of life does not really accept the child. His unacceptance is shown in his anxiety to spare and protect. So far as Job's righteousness is concerned, we may interpret the prologue as reaffirming the ancient axiom that virtue is not virtue until it has been tried. Does Job have to be privileged and protected, or does he too have a baptism of fire?

If, however, we see in the heavenly drama a God of dubious

[1] (Cleveland, Ohio: The World Publishing Company [Meridian Books], 1960.)

integrity, this is precisely the picture that Job has of God as a consequence of his sufferings. In words that are vivid with imagery, he repeatedly charges God not only with being unfair but also of being an outright sadist who delights in the sufferings he is arbitrarily inflicting upon the innocent.

The idea of fearing God for nought is in contrast to another line of thought in the Old Testament which maintains that God will reward those who fear him. If this seems to be a more primitive religious concept to the contemporary mind, it should be remembered that the Old Testament is vague concerning the life of the believer after death. Whatever assurance of justice that belief in God included had to be demonstrated in this present life. Because of the greater clarity regarding eternal life in the New Testament the believer can extend the opportunity for God's retributive justice into the life beyond. But the idea is the same.

To fear God for nought is something other. It is to affirm with almost nonsensical loyalty that regardless of what God does, I will not only remain faithful but even praise his name. This also is an Old Testament theme. "Though the fig tree do not blossom," says the prophet Habakkuk, "nor fruit be on the vines, the produce of the olive fail and the fields yield no food, the flock be cut off from the fold and there be no herd in the stalls, yet I will rejoice in the Lord, I will joy in the God of my salvation."

The greater clarity of the New Testament concerning the life beyond is no longer reflected in the New Testament community. With the coming of the *secular city,* we have arrived at full circle. We are back to the corporate personality of the Old Testament. The community of God is once again identified with the community of society. In exercising its stewardship of power, the church—or whatever the people of God choose to call themselves—is challenged to work within the corporate structures of the culture—economical, political, educational—to bring justice to the oppressed and the good life to the deprived. Once again the eschaton is confined to life on earth, and individual survival of death has little relevance. We have returned to a frame of reference in which we can understand the question, "Does Job fear God for nought?" as Job and his contemporaries understood it. Does human life have any meaning at all if justice is removed from the human scene? All cause and effect, all order and continuity, would then ultimately be an illusion. How then can we have hope? Job asks this question in a face-to-face confrontation with his own emptiness. "Where then," he asks, "is my hope?"

The outer catastrophes that Job experienced brought him much inner distress. These catastrophes are dramatically described in the sequence of "it never rains but it pours." First he experienced economic disaster—the loss of the oxen, asses, sheep, camels, and their attending servants. This was followed by a family disaster. Job's seven sons and three daughters, for whom it was his custom to offer sacrifices after their social affairs, were killed when a tornado struck their eldest brother's house where they were partying.

As Job held up under these ordeals, Satan asked for leave to afflict his body. The third catastrophe consequently was his health. Loathsome sores covered him from the sole of his foot to the crown of his head. The final catastrophe was his fall in prestige from a position of prominence in the community to becoming the butt of scoffers.

The effect of all these reversals produced yet another problem for Job—a religious problem—the nature of which is the substance of the book. In agony Job asks, "What has gone wrong between God and me? What kind of God is God to allow these things to befall me!"

Any sufferer recognizes his own inner anguish in the cries of Job against the injustice of the universe. None would question that his agony is commensurate with his calamities. Some may even feel guilty that they think at times just as Job does, but without the ostensible justification of Job's outer catastrophes. The Jobian protest—why!—is the natural reaction of the human spirit when the formulas and structures upon which one had counted begin to fail him. Job knew the religious formulas for the good life and now they seemed to be open mockeries. Small wonder that he would resent hearing these same formulas from the mouths of his three healthy friends. If you do your part, say the formulas, God will do his. But what happens when you do your part, as Job is convinced that he has, and everything goes to pieces even so!

2. RESPONDING vs. REACTING

Despite his overwhelming losses Job still had his wife and his three friends. Rather than being on the asset side of his ledger, however, they seem to constitute further debits. His wife obviously shared in the losses but vented her anger toward God upon Job. "Do you still hold fast your integrity?" she taunted. "Curse God, and die." Evidently she had counted on Job's privileged position before God and man for her own security, and in her despair over their fall, she could only despise him.

The three friends, Eliphaz, Bildad, and Zophar, came to visit Job with the best of intentions. They heard of his calamities and had made an appointment together to come to condole with him and comfort him. How better could one express a genuine pastoral motivation? We can scarcely expect that a pastor should recognize himself in these three physicians of the soul, since they are universally condemned for their ineptness. They are the "bad guys" in the drama, and who would choose to identify himself with such failures? Nor has the relationship inherent in the dialogues of these three been recognized for its pastoral significance. Yet it is precisely this response and reaction between the characters that provides us with our basis for the study of pastoral care.

The three friends are more like us than we naturally care to admit. They have acquired the bad habits that characterize many religious healers. Instead of functioning as physicians of the soul, they became defenders—defenders of God, of the church, of the Faith, of their role, of themselves. As a physician one is concerned with the hurt—how it may be healed. Yet like the three friends we are too often concerned about how the hurt is a threat to *us*. We become too egocentric then for a healing ministry where the self is identified with the needs of the other.

When these needs of the other are in the center of our attention, we *respond*. When on the other hand we are threatened by the needs of the other, we *react*. In responding we are drawn out of ourselves in identification with the other. In reacting we are preoccupied in defense as we are thrown back into ourselves by the threat in the situation.

By nature, human beings tend to flee pain and to seek comfort. So the pastor may flee the tense, negative, emotionally charged atmosphere of pastoral counseling for the comfort of conformity. Instead of being concerned with healing, he may be concerned that the person say the right thing or at least refrain from saying the wrong thing. We feel more safe with the *usual* and the *settled*.

In this manner we become prisoners of our own predispositions and captives to our culture. If I were to give one basic principle concerning what to say in any counseling situation, it would be to recall what our culture would consider the normal thing to say in such a situation and then to say the opposite. The same could have been said regarding the culture reflected by Job's three friends.

Like ours, the culture represented by the three friends is moralistic and rationalistic in character. Despite all our immorality, we still think in moral categories. We judge in terms of good or bad. Sex for all its openness is still looked upon as a titillating evil, and anger is still something we have difficulty in accepting.

Differences in viewpoint continue to threaten us, even in an acknowledgedly pluralistic society. We have an urge to straighten people out in their thinking. Pastors are prone to give accolades to those who speak in the religiously approved way and thus hold out their rewards for religious conformity as did the three friends. We eulogize what we want to hear and thus encourage the prospects of our hearing it. If the parishioner should say fine things about providence or prayer, the pastor may show his approval by saying even finer things. But what would he do if the parishioner were another Job and attacked rather than praised providence? Would he not react as did Eliphaz?

The three friends had a compulsive need to defend the ways of God as though they were defending themselves—and perhaps they were. The pastor may find his great difficulty in counseling when the subject turns to religion. He may identify God-language with his functional identity, since it is the language in which he preaches. When this language is injected into the counseling dialogue, he may lose his potential for responding and react instead with the party line. Should the Faith be attacked, he may feel his own role is attacked.

In this defensiveness the pastor like Job's three friends may have a compulsive need to maneuver the conversation to the positive. When he hears the Jobian lament from his parishioner, he feels the pressure to say, "Think how much worse off you could be!" Regardless of how black the sky is to his counselee, the defensive pastor is bent on finding a possible break in the clouds. The rather violent attack by many clergy upon Norman Vincent Peale for his therapy of positive thinking may have been a displaced attack on the clergy's own predisposition for the positive. Regardless of how objectively negative a pastor may view the contemporary scene, he may compulsively manipulate the conversation to the positive when he becomes involved in the emotionally charged atmosphere of a counseling relationship.

Because of his professional role, the pastor may find himself saying the trite and the expected thing as befitting his religious profession. In so doing he will sound like the three friends. The crucial issue is over how he envisions his function. Is he attempting to judge, to correct, to analyze, to say what he thinks a minister should say? His mental image of his role reveals whether he has other masters than Christ. If the Spirit would have us say something other than the expected, would he be able to get through the barrier of our own rigid mind set?

Like Eliphaz and his companions, we too may feel compelled to correct people when they say the religiously forbidden thing, because differences—particularly religious differences—are threatening. Our attempts to correct are usually on the rational level even though the differences expressed, as well as our reaction to these differences, may stem from emotional sources. When a person gives way as did Job to his negative feelings, we like Eliphaz may react negatively. Regardless of how we say it, what we mean is, "Now don't talk that way!" Sharing our culture's fear of hostility, we take expressions of anger personally, reacting defensively to resentment rather than responding in an understanding way. The negative frightens. We fear we cannot control its potential momentum.

Job's counselors are ominously similar to us all. They say the expected thing, react to stop threatening expression, and compulsively give a well-known religious answer to frustrations. They are unable to recognize the need of the sufferer simply to express his frustration. Their bad habits as counselors stemmed from the fact that they were bothered by Job and *reacted*. They lacked the courage to feel with Job and *respond*.

3. SACRAMENTAL SILENCE

What has been said about the ministry of the three friends refers only to the period "after Job opened his mouth." Prior to this moment, the story of their ministry was entirely different. Their beginning was in line with their pastoral purpose—to condole with him and comfort him. When they saw him, they were overcome with emotion, for Job's calamities had taken their toll on his appearance. They did not even recognize him. Giving expression to their immediate empathy, they raised their voices and wept, rent their robes, sprinkled dust on their heads toward heaven, and sat with him on the ground for seven days and seven nights. Yet they said nothing, for they saw that his suffering was very great.

Their empathetic silence, punctuated by the oriental gestures that signified deep feeling, was a symbolic response to Job's suffering. Though they spoke not a word, their symbolic silence spoke loud and clear. Theirs was a sacramental silence—a non-verbal and yet tangible communication of the spirit. Symbolic communication is dramatic and conveys more deeply at times than verbal communication. Most of us have had the experience of not knowing what to say when ministering to someone overcome with grief, and fortunately have had the good sense to say nothing. Our presence spoke for itself and was the basis for whatever words we may have said at a later time.

The three friends' ministry of silence has something to say to our talk-centered Western culture. One of my students raised the question whether we can take this account of such a prolonged ministry of silence with any credence. Fortunately, we had a Chinese student in our class who expressed his surprise that this question should even be raised. In the Orient, he said, the procedure of Eliphaz, Bildad, and Zophar is still practiced. When one is overtaken by misfortune, his friends visit him. Unlike the Westerner who visits only for a short period, the oriental friends may stay for days. Yet during this time they do not talk, for as the Chinese student said, "What is there to say?" Instead they feel with their friend, weep with him, and thus share his sorrow with him.

The sacramental silence of the three friends mediated a spirit of understanding to Job. He experienced the support of this empathy and was encouraged by it to speak from the heart. His words, consequently, were a contrast to the way the prologue describes his communication with his wife. When she told him to curse God and die, he reproved her. "Shall we receive good at the hand of the Lord, and shall we not receive evil?" he asked. Yet when Job opened his mouth to his three friends and broke the silence of the seven days, he cursed the day of his birth. It would appear that his wife's taunt had more effect on him than his retort to her would indicate. Yet in cursing the day of his birth, Job was not cursing God. His feelings toward God were far too complex for so simple a reaction.

III

THE JOBIAN BLAST AND ELIPHAZ' REACTION

Job 3–5

1. THE SUFFERER'S REAL FEELINGS

On the basis of the support implied by his friends' seven days and seven nights of symbolic concern, Job decided he could "open his mouth." In so doing he altered the whole course of the pastoral visit. "Sucked in" by the apparent empathy that was so dramatically though silently conveyed, Job felt he could share his real feelings. Unfortunately for all concerned, these feelings were very negative. Job cursed the day of his birth. Why, he asked, could he not have died the day he was born? His present catastrophe canceled the value of all his previous blessings. They were no compensation now for the sufferings he was enduring. His life had not been worth the effort.

In the prologue Job had resisted the temptation of his wife to curse God and die. Now he cursed the day of his birth and wished to die. Yet there is a difference. Job is more depressed than cynical. He is sick with despair—that sickness unto death of which Kierkegaard says the sufferer wishes to die but cannot.

Why, he laments, should life be given to the bitter in soul? Why can it not all cease with death and at least the misery come to an end? He cannot follow his wife's cynical directive because he cannot honestly curse God. His religious problem is not that simple. At the same time he cannot honestly defend God. His trauma seems too unfair. So he is caught in the middle and in anguish asks *why*.

Job's question *why* is more than a question. It is also a protest. As a question it is associated with guilt. What have I done to deserve all this? Is God punishing me for something? As a protest it expresses anger. Why is God picking on me! What kind of God would do such a thing? The *question* accepts the justice of God but as a *hidden* justice. The *protest* implies that God is unjust, and it challenges him to prove otherwise.

Job's question-protest *why* is the common reaction of the sufferer to his sufferings and disappointments. He simply cannot understand why such reversals in fortune are permitted to happen—and specifically why they happen to *him*. Whatever the sufferer had learned in his previous experiences about life and faith seems to be contradicted by the present reversal. The result is that he feels lost. With his former structure in collapse he is confronted by the despair of meaninglessness.

I have a friend who grew up in a pious farm family who believed very strongly that God would bless their endeavors if they worked hard and trusted in him. Each year this belief was tested and proved correct. If there was an occasional bad year, it was followed by several good years. Then came the successive years of drought. Hard work, trusting in God, and fervent prayer were all to no avail. Year followed year of crop failure. The financial crisis that ensued was matched by a religious crisis. What had gone wrong with the formula? Where was God in all this failure—and why?

C. S. Lewis is perhaps the most literate of recent Jobs. After the death of his wife, he experienced the full onslaught of the loss. In his little book *A Grief Observed* he gives expression to the questions and protests that stem from the agony of bereavement. "What chokes every prayer and every hope," he writes, "is the memory of all the prayers H. and I offered and all the false hopes we had. Not hopes raised merely by our own wishful thinking; hopes encouraged, even forced upon us. . . . Step by step we were 'led up the garden path.' Time after time when He [God] seemed most gracious, He was really preparing the next torture." [1] Lewis later described this lament as "a yell rather than a thought." Job also realized his lament was a yell. "The speech of a despairing man," he said, "is wind."

2. THE MORALIST IN ACTION

Eliphaz was shocked. He did not expect Job to have such feelings, let alone to express them so uninhibitedly. If Job would only have said what he did in the prologue, the three friends could have gone home relieved. He might have said, "Thank you for coming. I appreciate it. Yet I want you to know that God is good. Regardless of what is happening to me, I know his care is true and that I am in his hands." For this he could have received the highest pastoral compliment. "We came to comfort Job, but he comforted *us*. We received more than we gave."

But Job did not give the hoped-for testimony. Instead this stalwart man of faith cursed the day of his birth. What pastor would not have been thrown off balance by such despairing words from a respected parishioner? We ought to have no difficulty in understanding Eliphaz. Threatened by Job's blast,

[1] (Greenwich, Conn.: The Seabury Press, 1963), pp. 26-27.

he attempted—perhaps compulsively—to silence him. He took the approach of the moralist who tries to motivate people by making them feel guilty. Even his offer to respect Job's freedom is quickly retracted. "If one ventures a word with you, will you be offended? Yet who can keep from speaking?" His "speaking" could be summed up by saying, "Shame on you, Job! Why can't you practice what you've preached?"

Eliphaz' purpose is to shame Job into silence. If we can make a person feel guilty, we can control him. This is the most effective kind of domination because it is domination from within the person. By manipulating his conscience we can tyrannize his spirit. The rhetorical question is one of the tricks of this trade. "Is not your fear of God your confidence?" Eliphaz demands. The implication is clear. "Of course the fear of God is your confidence. Now don't talk so foolishly any more." Confronted with the rhetorical question, one is supposed to acknowledge his error and surrender.

Job's implied accusations against God's justice have irritated Eliphaz. In defense of God he affirms as axiomatic that God is just. The matter is simply not debatable. It was culturally assumed that God's ways were just, and one does not question cultural assumptions. Eliphaz even appeals to a religious experience of his own to support his point. It occurred in the dead of night. He felt a wind slide past his face and he trembled in dread. Although he could not distinguish anything definite, he could make out a form before him. Then a voice whispered, "Can mortal man be righteous before God?" The import—man is in no position to criticize the ways of God.

As further evidence, Eliphaz appeals to the angels—or saints. "To which of the holy ones—those with a reputation for godliness —can you turn for support?" he asks Job. All the spiritual authorities would agree that man reaps what he sows. The

28

justice of God is above suspicion. Although afflictions seem to be indigenous to human living—"man is born to trouble as the sparks fly upward"—the righteous will seek God and he will deliver them. On the basis of this argument, Eliphaz' advice to Job is to commit his cause to God and to trust in him.

His closing words are a testimony to God's trustworthiness. In this testimony there are some good thoughts which are similar even in wording to familiar biblical teachings regarding suffering. For example, Eliphaz says that a person is actually fortunate when God disciplines him by afflictions, because though he wounds, he also heals. This idea is also expressed in Proverbs and again in the Letter to the Hebrews. "The Lord disciplines him whom he loves, and chastises every son whom he receives." (Heb. 12:6.) Because it contains these insights into the chastening aspect of suffering, this section of Eliphaz' reaction is a selected Old Testament pericope for the sixteenth Sunday after Trinity.

The choice of this scripture as an Old Testament lesson raises a question concerning the influence of the context upon the words that are spoken. While Eliphaz spoke good words, he did so at the wrong time and in the wrong spirit. At a time when Job needed to let his feelings out, Eliphaz was attempting to silence him. When Job was primarily in need of understanding, Eliphaz was too threatened to give it. The question, then, is whether the right words spoken in the wrong spirit and at the wrong time are still the right words. Job did not think so, and I personally would agree.

For Eliphaz to counter Job's blast with the assurance that he is actually fortunate because God is disciplining him would be tantamount to a pastor quoting Romans 8:28 to a person in the throes of despair. Although the sufferer may have believed that "in everything God works for good with those who love him," he may also have the urge at that instant to strike the pastor.

"Talk to me about the truth of religion and I'll listen gladly," says the bereaved Lewis. "Talk to me about the duty of religion and I'll listen submissively. But don't come talking to me about the consolations of religion or I shall suspect that you don't understand." [2]

3. THE THERAPY IN EMPATHY

When the parents of six children lost their youngest in a fire, people tried to comfort them with the thought that they still had five children left. Commenting on this oft-heard condolence, the bereaved father said, "Somehow it didn't do much for us." It did not do much for them because it was spoken primarily to comfort the "comforter." The idea that they had five children made those who did not share the loss feel better about it.

Every loss is distinctive in itself. The shepherd in the Bible who had ninety-nine sheep in the fold was not comforted by this fact when he discovered one was lost. In all these misfortunes the sufferer focuses on what is lost, not on what is left. He does not view our words of comfort—whether they concern the five children who are left or even Romans 8:28—in the same perspective as does the would-be comforter. Instead of being consoled he may become angry. "It's easy for you to say that," he thinks, "because you don't know what it's like."

Eliphaz concludes his reaction to Job's blast with words that sound a great deal like Psalm 91. "He will deliver you from six troubles; in seven there shall no evil touch you," sounds like, "A thousand may fall at your side, ten thousand at your right hand; but it will not come near you." To Job all these fine words must have seemed bitterly inappropriate. Evil *had* touched him—in fact it had dealt him a blow that he thought was mortal. For

[2] *Ibid.*, p. 23.

one in Eliphaz' position, then, to say, "Lo, this we have searched out; it is true," must have seemed ironic. It was Job who was doing the searching, and perhaps also longing for a fellow sufferer who would search with him and relieve his isolation.

The notification of the death of their sons in the war in Vietnam came the same day to two families who lived within a short distance from each other in New York City. However, in the anonymity of metropolitan life they had never met each other. Nevertheless the father in one of the families expressed his desire to talk with the father in the other. "I want to talk with him," he said, "because he knows what it's all about."

Alcoholics Anonymous has made much of the principle that those who have gone through the same problems can best understand one another. The sober alcoholic knows how to talk to the alcoholic who needs sobering. The mutuality of their experience puts them on the same wave length. The pastor of a congregation can utilize this principle on a wider basis. He can make wise use of his parishioners who have known mental illness, marital problems, the loss of a mate, physical handicap, the shock of having a retarded child, and have come through these problems as a result of their faith. They can function as lay pastors under his direction to minister to those who have come upon similar straits. The empathy is there immediately and mutually.

Eliphaz gave Job the "whole load." Many of his points Job undoubtedly knew. Yet they no longer seemed relevant. They did not fit the situation as the sufferer alone would know it. Besides, Eliphaz' arguments ran counter to the protest in Job's lament. Behind his depression there was anger. Because he was threatened by this anger, Eliphaz only fanned its flames.

Yet he probably had the satisfaction of knowing that he had told Job what he needed to hear. He had done his duty. Things now should be settled and Job ought to conform. He no longer had any excuse. As we good people often say, "I've told him what to do. I've set him straight."

I am sure that Eliphaz felt he had spoken for God. But *had* he? He *defended* God. Yet as Kierkegaard has perceived, to defend God may be more a betrayal than an assist. "To defend anything," he said, "is always to discredit." In fact he who first invented the idea of defending God is "Judas No. 2." [3] Yet such defense is certainly no conscious betrayal. The pastor who feels obligated to set people straight may be following the principle articulated in Ezekiel for the watchman of Israel. If the watchman fails to warn the wicked of the evil of his ways so that he perishes in his iniquity, his blood will be required of the watchman. But if the watchman warns him, and he still does not turn from his wicked ways, the watchman is no longer responsible. His blood is on his own head.

When we say, "At least I've told him," we are implying we have fulfilled our responsibility. Yet this would be a very legalistic view of responsibility. Our concern, then, is more over having a good conscience than over helping the person and hence is more egocentric than pastoral. The pastor is also obligated to communicate *effectively*. It was said of the professors in a certain college that they had mastered the art of communicating their wisdom in the least effective way. What then happens to the rapport between teacher and student—between pastor and counselee? When Eliphaz permitted Job's cursing of the day of his birth to destroy his empathy for Job, he lost his most valuable potential for effective communication.

[3] *Sickness unto Death* (Garden City, N. Y.: Doubleday & Co., 1954), p. 218.

32

IV

THE JOBIAN OUTRAGE AND THE BILDAD ANSWER

Job 6–8

1. APPEAL FOR PITY

Eliphaz' reaction to Job's despair brings a counter reaction from Job. He is hurt by Eliphaz' lack of understanding. Although feeling he has been kicked when he was already down, his initial reaction is to weep rather than to become angry. Of course his words have been rash—if this is Eliphaz' objection. But who would not speak rashly under the circumstances? After all, the ass does not bray when he has enough food. Job is in pain. If his agony could be weighed, it would be heavier than the sand of the sea.

In appealing for Eliphaz' pity Job shows how defeated he really feels. In getting no sympathy from others, he feels sorry for himself. The pattern is a familiar one. His complaint over his lot irritates his "comforter" who then proceeds to admonish him; the comforter's rebuke is taken as rejection, and the sufferer dissipates into self-pity. Self-pity, however, is even more repulsive to the comforter than the initial complaint, and so the pattern perpetuates itself.

In lapsing into a pathetic plea for understanding, Job seems to have lost his spirit. He wants only to die. What can be the purpose of God's keeping him alive? Any meaning to his life is gone, and so why should he have to continue to exist—particularly when his existence is agony? But alas, this very agony is the sickness of which one cannot die. Unable to live and unable to die, Job "hits bottom." "In truth I have no help in me, and any resource is driven from me." He is "beat"—and therefore wide open for help. This is the moment which pastoral care has learned from the *Alcoholics Anonymous* to value—the potential *kairos* when all illusions of self-sufficiency are dispersed. It is Job's—and most sufferers'—first reaction when they get a full look not only at the scope but also at the hopelessness of their affliction.

2. SWITCH TO ATTACK

Having hit bottom, Job's mood changes. His disintegration in defeat ceases and he lashes out in attack upon Eliphaz. Did Eliphaz imply that he had forsaken the fear of God? Then let Eliphaz know that by his lack of empathy it is *he* who is guilty of such forsaking rather than Job. "He who withholds kindness from a friend forsakes the fear of the Almighty." An alternate reading would have Job insisting that he should have the kindness of his friends even though he *has* forsaken the fear of the Almighty. In either instance Job is making an accusation against Eliphaz.

What brought about this change in Job? If we use our imagination we could say that nonverbal as well as verbal communication was taking place between Job and the comforters. Perhaps after he had humbled himself into begging for pity, Job saw in the countenance of Eliphaz only contempt. Or he may have at least perceived that his humiliation was no more successful in stimulating empathy from Eliphaz than his complaint. Such cold indifference infuriated Job. Perhaps also the very experience of hitting bottom was in itself integrating. Under no more illusions about his situation, he was ready to cast off any restraint in his use of words.

Regardless of what precipitated this change from defeat to attack, Job continues on the offensive. His comforters are frauds! When they came to him they were as promising as an oasis to the tired desert caravan. As one parched with thirst from the desert of his own afflictions, Job reached out for their proffered relief. But then at the moment of contact to discover that the promised oasis was a mirage! What a horrible disappointment and utter disillusion! "Such you have now become to me!"

Job does more than denounce Eliphaz as a fraud. He tells him why his counseling is a failure. "You see my calamity, and are afraid." This is a remarkable insight on the part of Job into the conflict of his comforter. Many of us experience anxiety in the presence of those who have experienced tragedy. The anxiety is caused by more than our empathy. It is due also to a sense of guilt in having been spared. Why he and not I? We assume the bereaved is asking the same question. And what is the answer? There simply is none. Hence we are anxious.

The better we know the people upon whom tragedy strikes, the more we feel the shock. It is a relief to discover that those involved are strangers. The affair slips more easily then from our remembrance. There is a natural reluctance to experience the pain of tragedy—especially our own but also in empathy with others. The manager of the Hilton Hotel in Chicago refused to allow the wounded Viet-Nam veterans from a nearby hospital to see his floor show while other patrons were present. These patrons, he said, dislike being reminded of tragedy when they have paid for entertainment. These patrons, of course, knew that wounded soldiers were in the area government hospital. But as long as they were removed from the situation—as long as they were not in the actual presence of these veterans—they could dismiss the tragedy from their minds.

Yet our very failure to empathize in the pain of others can make us feel guilty. Our reactions to this guilt are varied. Some accept their guilt as a reprimand and compensate by demonstrating their concern in obvious ways. Through their involvement they are saying, "See, I care very much." Others react by seeking to fault the sufferer. Perhaps some of this was his own fault. Through their judgments they are saying, "It is not necessary for me to feel guilty because some of this is his own fault." In either instance the person is anxious over the situation. Eliphaz' reluctance to empathize with Job's despair was his defense against the guilt and fear that were activated by Job's tragedy. "You see my calamity and are afraid."

3. ANGER FROM HUMILIATION

Job's blast at Eliphaz expressed the feelings of the forsaken. In his sufferings he had begged for sympathy. Eliphaz' hardness had forced him into such degradation that he was humiliated. Was what he had asked really so unreasonable? As Job himself put it, "Have I said, . . . 'From your wealth offer a bribe for me,' or, 'Deliver me from the adversary's hand'?" All he had asked for was empathy, and even this was too much for Eliphaz.

The very position of begging into which the sufferer is placed creates a backlash of hostility. Normally, however, he is not in a position to show this hostility. He does not want to lose what little contact he still has with his "friends." Also his very suffering continues to preoccupy his attention. He is too much in need to be hostile. But afterward—when the suffering subsides—the hostility comes to the fore.

This phenomenon can be observed in "restored" romances and in "reconciled" marriages. The lover whose persistence and even pleading has been hard on his self-respect may nevertheless finally persuade his reluctant sweetheart to resume the relationship. The erring mate whose abject pleas and promises have been the equivalent of "eating crow" may still move the offended partner to relent and forgive. After all is well again, however, the restored sweetheart may show his appreciation by breaking the romance himself and the forgiven partner may begin to act indifferently toward his mate. While each received what he so desperately wanted by his begging, his self-respect was outraged in the process. The hate that springs from humiliation is momentarily set aside by the distress of the moment but will often erupt when this distress subsides. The need then is to retaliate by turning the tables on the other person.

Although Job is still very much in his distress, his begging has come to nought. Having nothing to lose from his three friends, he lets go with his hostility in the midst of his desperation. Once he has taken to the offensive, he presses his attack. Since Eliphaz has been critical, let him be specific concerning Job's faults. Job insists he is open to any honest confrontation. But the sort of moralistic reproof that Eliphaz has given, Job can only disdain. In fact this is precisely why Eliphaz has failed as a counselor. Instead of understanding the emotional nature of Job's despair, he held him to a rational account of his words. Job sees the error clearly. "Do you think that you can reprove words, when the speech of a despairing man is wind?"

The counselor who operates on a rational level with an emotional outburst is failing to respond. Eliphaz could not communicate with Job because he could not adapt himself to the emotional level of Job's discourse. Hence they were on different frequencies. This is a common tendency for pastors when they are confronted without warning by an outburst of negative emotion. The counselor becomes instinctively defensive. He reacts hostilely out of fright and takes literally the overcharged words of a despairing soul. He lacks the courage to take these feelings into himself. To Job Eliphaz is just plain cruel. Not only is he the kind of person who would "cast lots over the fatherless," he would even "bargain over a friend."

Although the two men were obviously missing each other in their communication, Job made a further attempt to get on common ground. Let us agree at least, he persists, that this is a pretty rough world. Man is like a slave who longs even for a little shade, or like a hireling who lives only for his meager wage. Naturally Job was looking at life through the blackness of his own despair. Because this black perspective was so real to him, he assumed Eliphaz has to acknowledge its validity. Life for Job is simply "months of emptiness." Though Tillich sees the anxiety of emptiness and meaninglessness as dominant in our own age, ancient Job experienced it to the full. Even the nights offer no respite. He tosses and turns waiting for the dawn. There are no longer nights than those in which one cannot sleep. Yet when the night is finally over, what does the new day hold for him? Simply more emptiness of soul and misery of body, as his skin hardens only to break out again while the worms infest his sores.

Because of the accumulation of sleepless nights and empty days, Job's negative feelings have pre-empted his powers of reason. He is emotionally distraught, and behind his hostility there is panic. It is the panic of hopelessness in the face of death. All of Job's losses—his children, his property, his status, and his health—are symbols of the ultimate loss of life in death. Behind Job's anxiety over the emptiness of his life is his anxiety over fate and death.

Job's desire of death and his simultaneous fear of it are comparable to his paradoxical perception of time. For Job, time both "drags" and "flies." Even as his sleepless nights seem endless, so his empty days are "swifter than a weaver's shuttle" for they show no progress. This paradox concerning the passing of time is common to the experience of the sufferer. Time hangs heavy because normal activity is curtailed. Yet the days of suffering succeed one another with unbelievable speed. The ominous fear behind Job's ambivalence over time is that his days are "coming to their end without hope." When hope no longer abides, all structure to life, including the time structure, collapses.

In the absence of hope Job finds a morbid satisfaction in his approaching death. He warns the three friends and later even God that the time is coming when they will behold him no more. Since he cannot evoke any pity while living, perhaps he can at least evoke some guilt when dead. Most of us have known those times when we felt totally misunderstood and unappreciated. The child often feels this way in regard to his parents. When he is crushed by what he interprets as a complete resistance to his needs, he may compensate by imagining his corpse in a coffin with mother and father weeping over his bier. "Oh, how I wish we had treated the poor little fellow better while he yet lived," they lament. So warns Job, "Thou wilt seek me, but I shall not be." Someday you'll be sorry!

4. DIRECT TO GOD

In the meantime Job must live on in hopelessness. His desperation moves him to enunciate his disregard for any precaution in what he says. He has no intention of restraining his mouth from expressing his bitterness of soul and anguish of spirit. Further-more he will recognize his chief antagonist as God and not Eliphaz. He will no more hold back his words to please God than to please the three friends. What has he to lose in letting go with his hostility—even with God? Who is it that has destroyed his hope of finding respite at least in sleep? Is it not God who has disrupted his sleep with terrifying dreams? God get off my back! Why do you persist in keeping me alive just to torture me?

In words that sound like the eighth psalm but have a reverse intention, Job accuses God of picking on him. Instead of asking, "What is man that thou art mindful of him, and the son of man that thou dost care for him?" he demands, "What is man, that thou dost make so much of him . . . let me alone till I swallow my spittle." Why am I so important to you that you keep tormenting me, giving me no reprieve even to swallow?

Like other sufferers Job cannot understand why God has singled him out. In words reminiscent of his own spiritual torment, Luther describes the person in despair as wishing that "God were not God, so that he might not suffer such things from him." [1] Eliphaz has implied that Job's sin is the possible cause of God's attention. But this Job cannot buy. Speaking indirectly to Eliphaz but directly to God, he demands to know why his transgressions should be so important. How could his puny little sins be of any great moment to God? And if his sin is such an issue, why does not this "watcher of men" forgive him instead of rubbing it in!

In a sense Job's words to God, angry as they are, are similar to his opening words to Eliphaz. In asking, "Why are you pick-ing on me—making such a special case of me?" he is indirectly

[1] Gordon Rupp, *The Righteousness of God* (New York: Philosophical Library, 1953), p. 112.

appealing to God's pity. Job feels that he has become a target for God's arrows; he wants to know why—why *me!*

5. BILDAD THE OVERSIMPLIFIER

Job's audacity in challenging God brings in the second comforter. While all three of these comforters have much the same point of view, each has his own personal distinction. If Eliphaz is a moralizer, Bildad is an oversimplifier. He has some pity for Job and hence is the most compassionate of the three. He offers a simple solution amidst his accusations. Bildad enters the fray by using Job's admission of rashness as a club to pummel him into silence. "So you acknowledge your words are windy! How long then are you going to keep this big wind blowing?" Obviously Job's appeal for understanding had missed its mark on Bildad. Like Eliphaz he simply could not accept an emotional outburst with compassion. The threat inherent in rashness could evoke only reproof.

Like Eliphaz, Bildad also resorted to the rhetorical question to bring Job to compliance. "Does God pervert justice?" Obviously the purpose of the question is to bring forth an inevitable *no* from Job. Of course God is not unjust—shame on me for even implying it! Believing Job would be afraid to answer yes to this question, Bildad was seeking a quick end to the argument by silencing his opponent. The use of the question to intimidate is the weapon of the moralist. The moralist has a system of rigid boundaries to the freedom which he will tolerate. The rhetorical question is the electrified charge from the boundary fencing to drive the erring back into the safer limits. The questioner is counting upon the person's having the latent fear and guilt that will make his tactic effective.

Once Bildad had resorted to intimidation, he let go with a low blow. We know from the prologue that Job had his worries over his children. When they had their parties, he offered sacrifices for them lest they had sinned and cursed God. Now these children were dead. But Bildad rubs the sensitive area. "If your children have sinned against him, he has delivered them into the power of their transgression." In the heat of the argument he could not resist letting Job know that others were aware of his children's wild oats. And again the cause and effect is evident: they were killed in the tornado because of their sin. On this basis Bildad offered Job his simple formula.

a. "If you will seek God
b. And make supplication to the Almighty,
c. If you are pure and upright,
d. Surely then he will rouse himself for you and reward you with a rightful habitation."

To support his position, Bildad—again like Eliphaz—appeals to the fathers. "Consider what the fathers of bygone ages have found. Will they not teach you what Eliphaz and I have been trying to impress upon you?" Bildad seemingly cannot comprehend that such an appeal to the authority of tradition would not be decisive. Consequently the best he can do is to resort to repetition.

Though the formula is simple, it is not to be taken lightly. Bildad's counseling could be called Bildad's warning. If you take the reed away from its marshy habitat, how long will its flower last and its leaves remain unwithered? The same fate awaits him—Job, note well!—who forgets God. There is absolutely no escape from such a fate. When he leans against his house, it will not stand. Should he wish to return, it will be too late. His own place will say, "I have never seen you."

Bildad concludes his appeal by exhorting Job to cooperate. Then all sorts of good things will take place! God will "fill your mouth with laughter, and . . . those who hate you will be clothed with shame." One might even see this as a bit of bribery: You have been rash, Job, and of course you shouldn't have been. But just see the light now and conform, and we'll forget the past and all will be well. The thunder has abated and the counselor is now patronizingly cajoling the naughty boy. Be a good fellow, Job, and everything will be all right. Go along with us and you'll see—it pays! Less gifted than Eliphaz, Bildad appears to be a simple fellow, not too bright or reflective. But perhaps also in his limitations—or even because of them—a bit more compassionate.

V

THE JOBIAN LASH AND
THE ZOPHAR ATTACK

Bildad's concluding touch of concern, patronizing though it was, may have moved Job. He acknowledges that God will not reject a blameless man. Yet this is small comfort, for how can any man be blameless before God? As Jesus said, "No one is good but God alone" (Mark 10:18). Job, however, is concerned more with God's arbitrariness than with God's goodness. Man is more trapped than he is sinful. Job consents to the familiar expressions of God's transcendental sovereignty—that he has created all that exists and is accountable to no one, that he does great things that are beyond our understanding, even to commanding the sun and sealing up the stars. On this issue Job will give his friends no argument. But then he cracks the whip! It is precisely Gods' transcendental sovereignty that incenses him. Since God is so "wholly other," who then can reach him even in desperation? If one wished to contend with him, the odds are so infinitely uneven that he would not stand a chance. "One could not answer him once in a thousand times." Who can prevent him from doing what he wants? Who would even dare to ask him, "What doest thou?"

1. NO BARGAINING POWER

Because God is transcendent and sovereign, Job feels he is in a hopeless predicament. How can you argue with such a God? "Though I am innocent, I cannot answer him." He can only appeal for mercy to him whom he considers his accuser! If the contest is a matter of strength, God wins before it begins. If it is a matter of justice, who can call God to account? All is so futile! Though Job believes he is innocent, he has no confidence that he could defend his innocence before God. "My own mouth would condemn me." Though he believes he is blameless, he is convinced that this sovereign God would somehow "prove him perverse." He is beat before he starts simply because God is God and Job is only a man.

There is nothing particularly ancient about Job's charge that life is unfair. The modern sufferer may express this same feeling to an acceptive pastor. Yet there may be something ancient about Job's conclusion that an unfair life means an unfair God. In our day the pastor hears more doubts about God's existence than about his fairness. In all his doubting Job seems never to question that God *is*. The question, rather, is over God's *character*. Where modern man says, "This is a lousy world," Job says, "I have a lousy God." Perhaps the cultural difference—if there is one—is more in wording than in actual religious content. Perhaps what we really mean when we say, "This is a lousy world," is "We have a lousy God." Yet in our thought forms a lousy world is more indicative of no God than a lousy God. Where we say, "How can there be a God in a world like this?" Job says, "A world like this must have a devious God."

Perhaps we have oversimplified this difference. Our contemporary Job, C. S. Lewis, like the ancient Job, questions in his despair not God's existence but his character. In the midst of his grief he writes "Not that I am (I think) in much danger of ceasing to believe in God. The real danger is of coming to believe such dreadful things about Him. The conclusion I dread is not 'So there's no God after all,' but 'So this is what God's really like. Deceive yourself no longer.'" [1] In coming into belief after years of unbelief, Lewis would not be a typical doubter. Yet we still must ask whether something other than a cultural difference may be involved in this inclination to doubt God's goodness rather than his existence. Lewis, like Job, had a meaningful relationship with God *prior* to his bereavement. When such is the case the tragedy may seem more like a betrayal of this relationship than an exposure of it as an illusion. Hence the hostility toward such a Deceiver.

Job counters Bildad's rhetorical question "Does God pervert justice?" by a defiant *yes!* He will not be silenced by such bull-dozing tactics. He will not quail before the charge of blasphemy. God destroys both the blameless and the wicked. In fact the earth is given into the hand of the wicked while God mocks at the calamity of the innocent. Job climaxes his devastating indict-ment of God by challenging Bildad to produce an alternate cul-prit. "If it is not God who then is it?"

This is a good question—a question that pastoral counselors must have the courage to face. At the funeral of two young teen-agers from the same family killed in a tragic accident, the minister said, "God did not do this." I do not say that he did. Yet I ask with Job, "If it is not God, who then is it?" If we cannot conceive of a good God doing such tragic things, how about a devil God? If neither of these alternatives is satisfactory, have we an impotent God? Does he—like us—remain helpless before these catastrophes? Is his grief like our grief? If he cannot prevent them, is he really God? What, then, does trusting

[1] *A Grief Observed*, pp. 9-10.

46

in him mean? If he could prevent them but does not, how then can we defend him from Job's charges?

2. THE LONGING FOR CONTACT

In casting off all restraint Job revealed the depth of the religious problem that has been created by his tragic losses. He sees no way out. He had tried to "talk turkey" to himself—telling himself to snap out of it, to get hold of himself, to forget it, to smile, at least to act as if he were in good spirits. In so doing he anticipated the familiar advice that comforters sooner or later give to the despairing. But for Job the problem was too dangerous to forget and too serious to ignore. "If I say, 'I will forget my complaint, I will put off my sad countenance, and be of good cheer,' I become afraid of all my suffering, for I know thou wilt not hold me innocent." Behind Job's defiance is the awful fear that his troubles really *do* indicate that he is guilty or at least that before God he is bound to be judged undone. I heard a chaplain in a general hospital say that when he visits a patient he tries to help that person think of himself as a good person. When people are afflicted, he said, they inevitably begin to wonder whether their affliction is a punishment from God. The logical conclusion from such thoughts is that they must be wicked persons. As a bearer of good news the chaplain believed he should communicate to such sufferers that their sufferings do not indicate that they are bad. He approached the issue from the positive, however, by helping them to see themselves as good.

Yet his pastoral care has to go deeper than mere *telling*. The sufferer, like Job, has a sense of doom, particularly if he is an older person. This hopelessness is rooted in a conscience that has wrestled with guilt before, but under the weight of physical affliction is unable any longer to withstand the indictment. "If

I wash myself with snow, and cleanse my hands with lye, yet thou wilt plunge me into a pit, and my own clothes will abhor me." The sufferer is like a child who in family troubles may resist his parents and blame them for his unhappiness, and yet in the depths of his own being actually is blaming himself. Outwardly he says, "What's wrong with my parents?" but inwardly he says, "What's wrong with *me?*" Such self-blame is the inevitable conclusion of any dependent person when in conflict with his environment. Whether he is dependent because he is a child or because he is afflicted like Job, he is by his very dependency "on the bottom." The only way he can look outward is to look upward. The *powers that be* are on top of him and seem destined by an arbitrary fate ultimately to be *right*.

As Job takes the doctrine of divine transcendence to its blind alley in human frustration, he expresses for the first time a longing for a mediator. The gulf between man and God is so infinite that his only hope for encounter is for some sort of "go-between" who "might lay his hand upon us both." If there were such a man, Job could take his case before him. But the very dread inherent in any confrontation with a transcendent and sovereign God is enough to terrify him. If God wants to be fair, let him take away this dread—put aside his rod—and then Job could feel free enough to speak. For Job's desire—his real longing —is to be able to take his case directly to God. For this to be possible, the dread implicit in the gulf between them has to be removed.

3. JUST A LITTLE PEACE

After expressing so very clearly why he could not speak as he would like to God, Job seems to have found some release from his fear. Since he loathed his life anyhow, why should he not give free utterance to his complaint? What need had he to conform or to please since he is beyond being helped? Why should he not let God have it right between the eyes? The least that God could do is to let him know why he has become Job's adversary! Having nothing to lose, Job for the first time unleashes his attack on God *to* God. "Does it seem good to thee to oppress, to despise the work of thy hands and favor the designs of the wicked?"

Job's boldness is indicative of his growing strength. His anger is taking over and although not a constructive force in itself, anger is at least a force. Nor is his attack without rational reflection. Why, he asks God, do you search for my sin when you know that I am not guilty and that there is no one to deliver me when you pick on me! Why did you create me in the first place if now all you plan to do is destroy me? What sense is there in such contradictory pursuits? You are the One that made me—knitting me together with bones and clothing me with flesh—and gave me life and, yes, even cared for me and preserved me. At this point Job seems momentarily to lose himself in the memory of his previous relationship with God. There is a touch of tenderness here, even if nostalgic. After his blast at God has been spent, Job evidently experiences a new confidence in God. Yet its sharp contrast with his present misery makes his recall of the past of short duration. God becomes again the devil God. All the while he was being good to Job, he was simply setting him up for the fall. Rather than the frowning providence hiding a smiling face, the smiling face was hiding a frowning providence. The momentary hope was an illusion.[2]

Job is caught in the circle of inevitable despair. The good past only makes God more of a betrayer. Whether Job has been wicked or righteous is of little moment. God was going to get

[2] Cf. *The Anchor Bible, Job,* p. 78.

him one way or another. He is like a lion who is stalking his prey with a relentless and ever increasing hostility. So what's the use? Here is the dead end to all his reflection—the betrayal of trust that pulls back to itself like a magnet any hope that would soar beyond it. Why all the bother, God? "Why did you bring me forth from the womb? Would that I had died before any eye had seen me."

Was Eliphaz shocked because Job had dared to curse the day of his birth? Then let him have a bigger shock as Job curses the day of his birth directly to God. Looking back over his life and facing only death in the future, Job wishes that he could have avoided the conscious experience of both. Because of all that has happened to whatever was good in his life, he wishes now that he could have been "carried from the womb to the grave." For whatever of life is yet before him, he has but one request that he hopes will be granted—"Let me alone!" Since the days that remain for me are of necessity few, could I at least have a little comfort before I go whence I shall not return? God—get off my back for just a little while! For other than a temporary relief I can hope for nothing ahead but "the land of gloom and deep darkness."

One reason why the Book of Job is a help in pastoral care is that Job speaks for the sufferers of all ages and places, including our own. As unusual as his request for a little peace before entering into the darkness of death may appear, it is not unusual for a sufferer in Job's mood of despair. The following pastoral account of a modern Job is an example of this frame of mind. He was a prisoner in a state penitentiary and the following excerpt is from the fourth visit by the pastor. During the previous session the prisoner had expressed the hope that his estranged wife would visit him. Instead he received a notice that she had filed divorce papers. The pastor was not aware of this development as the visit began. Although he had profited from a study of the Book of Job and refrained for the most part from succumbing to the common tendency to be Eliphaz, the prisoner's desire for a little peace before he "descended to the Pit" proved too much for him.

Pastor: Good to see you again, J. How are things going today?

J: Hi! (smiled.) OK, same as usual. Say, I got transferred to the tailor shop.

P: Oh?

J: Yeah. Nothing goes right for me, it's always been that way. I don't know anything about that. Now I just sit around.

P: How do you like it? (resistance to hearing the negative.)

J: It's OK, but I don't do anything.

P: I see.

J: I'm single now. Wednesday I got the final divorce papers. (smiled and paused.)

P: I understood that she was coming up to see you and together you would try to work things out.

J: That's what my mother said. She was coming up the first chance that she got and that she would write. The only letter that I got from her is the divorce. The only thing to do now is to forget her.

P: Forget?

J: Yeah, just forget that I ever knew her.

P: That will be hard to do.

J: Yah. (pause.)

P: All this was quite a blow to you.

J: It sure was. You know all my life is this way; once I get feeling good something comes along and kicks the props out from under me and I'm back down again. Some guys get all the breaks and I try but it just doesn't come my way.

P: You never seem to get the breaks.

J: That's for sure. I don't pray to God anymore. He can't be just when I try and yet he doesn't help me. I don't care, but from now on it's just me.

P: You'll play it alone.

J: Yeah. Nothing goes right for me, it's always been that way. I wish that someone would put me under. If I had the guts to do it, I would do it myself. (pause.) I tried it once but I didn't cut deep enough. That was when I was in the county jail. Too bad it failed. (long pause.)

P: Things are unbearable.

J: Never does anything go right. I was even thinking about going over the wall. Got a 50-50 chance.

P: A 50-50 chance?

J: Sure, 50 that I get over and 50 that I don't. If I made it, I sure wouldn't come back here. You have to be smarter than they are so that you don't be caught. They wouldn't get me (pause) because if they did, I'd have to spend the total time and that's too much. And if I didn't get over the wall, there's the other chance.

P: That's a big change. (resistance.)

J: True, but if they did shoot me that would be OK; then I'd have no more worries.

P: But where would you go if you were killed? (once started, hard to stop.)

J: I know where I'd go and that'd be down.

P: That doesn't worry you. (Eliphaz is in the wings.)

J: No.

P: You know what the Bible says about hell. (entrance, Eliphaz.)

J: Sure. But that's where I'll go.

P: Spending eternity in suffering doesn't bother you. I thought that you had enough suffering. Are you willing to take that chance?

J: Well, you see, I figure that just before I go down, I'll have a few minutes of peace. (Job 10:20-21.)

P: I understand your feelings, but are a few minutes of peace worth suffering forever in hell?

J: I don't know. I just want to get away from all these problems. I can't seem to get there. Ending it would not solve any problems. Talking it over sure has helped. But I still can't see God as being a just God. Anyway, right now I can see no use in prayer.

4. GUILT OR MEANINGLESSNESS

Eliphaz and Bildad concentrated on guilt as the source of Job's problem while Job concentrated on the meaninglessness and emptiness of life. If Job could agree with his friends about his guilt, he would no longer be preoccupied with the meaninglessness of life. Guilt implies that life has meaning—that there is a standard which is larger than the individual. When the individual transgresses this standard, he experiences the justifiable consequences. Perhaps we tend to perpetuate our guilt because of this and other advantages that it offers. Though guilt is miserable, we can grow accustomed to it. It offers the "security of the familiar." We are at home with it. Besides, were we to give it up, we might be confronted with the anxiety of meaninglessness. The virgin territory of guiltlessness has no stakes or boundary lines indicating a familiar pattern. Since we are used to the anxiety of guilt, the anxiety of meaninglessness may seem the greater of the two miseries. To protect ourselves from the threat of the unknown—the perils of meaninglessness—we may hold tenaciously to the security of the known—the discomfiture of guilt.

For Job to admit to guilt would have been to surrender his honesty. At the expense of his own security, he can admit only to an irrational guilt. He feels doomed to judgment not because he is aware of any transgressions, but only because his God is capricious in his transcendence. This kind of guilt, however, puts no meaning into life, for it is guilt outside the realm of human freedom. Job feels no responsibility for it; rather he feels trapped by it. There is no pattern of consistency that he can follow. Whether he is innocent or guilty, his judgment is the same.

This view of God corresponds to the way Jung sees the God of Job. Job had wished that God were a man so that he could present his case to him. But his God is beyond such appeals. He is not ethically accountable to anyone. In fact Job is more ethically conscious than God. Yet Job's demands upon God have found their way into God's consciousness. Instead of God testing Job, God was actually testing himself. He was projecting upon Job his own doubts about his own integrity. Now that Job had made his case clear, God's answer to Job could no longer be the simple affirmation of his sovereignty. Like Job himself, Jung believes that a mediator must come. For Jung this mediator has come in the person of Christ. God had to become man to endure as man what he had inflicted upon his servant Job. In no other way could he bring peace to his own disturbed conscience. By enduring as man what Job endured at God's hand, God has come to terms with the ethical demands implicit in Job's complaint.

5. THE ANGRY ONE

Job's lash at Bildad brings in the third "comforter." According to Eastern propriety, Zophar as the youngest of the three probably had to wait until the other two had spoken. At any rate he was "champing at the bit" to enter the fray. When one desires to speak but lacks the opportunity, he may come in "with both feet" once he gets the chance. Zophar's urge to hit Job was doubled in intensity by the irritating delay. He is the *angry one.*

Zophar begins by sarcastically referring to Job's lament as a multitude of words and to Job as a man full of talk. He, like Bildad, takes up Job's point that the speech of a despairing man is as wind, and uses it against him. Do you think that because you are full of wind, we should be silent before you? Are you to be vindicated simply because of your multitude of words? Whatever hope Job had of evoking sympathy from these men was now gone. Zophar's purpose is plain. "When you mock, shall no one shame you?" Job's reaction to his tragedy is for Zophar a pure mockery of the sacred. Shame upon him! But Job is not ashamed and therefore Zophar's course is clear. By his own admission his goal is to shame him.

Job's insistence that he was clean in his own eyes infuriated Zophar. Such impudence in the presence of God should not go unpunished. "Oh, that God would speak and open his lips to you." Oh, that God would do what we three friends seem unable to do—bring you to your knees!

Zophar expresses the familiar anger of the "righteous" toward the "sinner." When the "sinner" appears to be getting away with his sin, the "righteous" are incensed. Like the disciples John and James who were angered by the Samaritan village that refused to receive Jesus because he was headed toward Jerusalem, they want to call down fire from heaven upon the offender. When a high school Sunday school class discussed the efforts of atheist Madeline Murray to eliminate religious symbols from public life, one of the girls said vehemently, "She ought to have a hole put in her head."

What is it that angers the righteous when the mockers express themselves? Is it their love for the Lord? Not if love for the Lord is part and parcel with love for people—as the Lord himself said it was. Also it was the Lord who rebuked his angry disciples for their desire to call down the fire. Anger is more often an expression of fear than of love. If the sinner persists unchallenged, he shakes the ladder under the righteous. Since their God is sovereign, their security lies in conforming to him. If mockers are unrestrained, God's sovereignty is open to question. What happens then to the security of the righteous? Hence their anger—violent anger—toward the mocker.

Like most of us when we are incensed, Zophar is not concerned about being temperate. Rather he is concerned about landing a quick haymaker. Swinging from the floor, he flails wildly at his "opponent": So you resented it when Eliphaz and Bildad inferred that your sufferings were commensurate with your guilt! Then listen to *me*. "Know then that God exacts of you less than your guilt deserves." In other words, Job, you are getting a bargain!

Zophar thought he had good reason for making such a charge. He had the advantage over Eliphaz and Bildad in that he had heard Job defy each of them. Any man who talks as Job did—who mocks without shame—is simply not a good man. He is fortunate to be still alive, let alone able to talk. How God could restrain himself from striking Job dead is beyond Zophar. In fact, he would probably have felt more secure in his own faith if God would not have restrained himself.

In spite of the intensity of his attack, Zophar still follows the route of the other two. After his attack, he pointed, as did they, to God's transcendence. Who can restrain such a sovereign God when he sees those who are evil? Yet there is a formula for escape—even for Job. "If you will set your heart aright—if guilt is in your hand, remove it." Like the others Zophar waxes eloquent about the reward for such conformity. "Your life will be brighter than the noonday; . . . you will have confidence; . . . you will be protected." But his closing is a warning. "The eyes of the wicked will fail; all way of escape will be lost to them, and their hope is to breathe their last." This is what Zophar wants to believe. Yet as Job defies "the system" Zophar is shaken. The degree to which he is shaken is shown by the vehemence of his attack.

VI

THE DEEPENING CLEAVAGE

1. HIT BACK IN ANGER

Zophar's angry attack left Job even more defiant. Instead of shaming him into submission, it evoked further resentment. Job's rising hostility appears to strengthen him. It serves as an integrating power that enables him to affirm himself before his three friends. Zophar's attack brought a sarcastic counterattack. "No doubt you are the people, and wisdom will die with you." He refuses to bow before the arrogance of his comforters. He reminds them that he has understanding as well as they. The points upon which they are hammering—who does not know them? They are the well-worn religious dogmas in which all of them were reared. He will not be "talked-down-to." "I am not inferior to you."

The integrating effect of anger is recognized in many areas of life. When a sick person becomes crotchety, we often conclude that he is getting better. A coach may deliberately rile his phlegmatic team in order to integrate its determination. Frank Torre, former major league baseball player, provoked his obese younger brother Joe by calling him "fat boy" in public. Realizing that

Joe had the potential for the big leagues, he also knew he would never make it unless he controlled his weight. So he needled him mercilessly. Joe admits that during those days he hated the brother he also admired. Yet Joe Torre became the top catcher in the major leagues.

This same phenomenon may occur in the pastoral ministry to dependent people. An example is a middle-aged woman who had a history of chronic lethargy and withdrawal. She was a burden to her husband and he simply assumed her responsibilities as the easier way. Finally he realized that she was becoming more than he could endure. In conference with the pastor he decided that if she was unable to function because of her mental problems, he would have to commit her to a mental hospital. Although the husband was reluctant, the pastor encouraged him to tell his wife what he had decided. The woman reacted to the news with the first vitality that she had shown in years. Furious that he would do such a thing to her, she berated him with verbal abuse. When the pastor called, she was at first coldly polite, but when he acknowledged her husband's decision, she let her hostility go against him also. He accepted it but remained firm. This marked the beginning of a recovery that is now of several years duration. Evidently the woman needed this confrontation with reality, and her angry reaction to it was the beginning of her self-affirmation.

I myself have never evoked anger from a counselee as a premeditated strategy. I have, however, evoked such anger without premeditation. There are those times in counseling when one becomes resistive to a counselee's repeated laments and confronts him rather bluntly about his responsibilities. This has at times evoked shock from the counselee and then anger. Yet in every instance which I can recall, the anger seemed to be a strengthening influence. For some it was actually the turning point toward maturity—even if their motivation was simply their determination to show me that they were not as weak and dependent as I had thought.

2. HOW THE MIGHTY HAVE FALLEN

Job feels that his calamity has made him the laughingstock of his friends. There is nothing fair about what has happened to him. He, a God-fearing man, has suffered such reversals while robbers, idolaters, and God-defiers remain secure and at peace. Job feels he is despised simply because he has had misfortune. The trap from which he cannot escape is that his very calamity is the indication to others that he is evil and therefore subject to abuse.

No doubt some of Job's description of his social rejection is his own projection of self-contempt. When one has suffered a setback, his sense of self-worth also suffers, and he may actually provoke the kind of reaction from others that confirms his suspicions. Yet there is also a very real tendency for people to kick a person when he is down. "In the thought of one who is at ease," says Job, "there is contempt for misfortune." Such misfortune to others disturbs his justification for being at ease himself. If he is to preserve his justification, he must find reason to pass judgment upon the one "whose feet have slipped." In a scene from the motion picture *The Days of Wine and Roses,* a young alcoholic in desperation for a drink attempted to steal liquor from a tavern. The proprietor, however, overtook him and in the ensuing struggle sadistically emptied the contents of the bottle on the alcoholic's face as the unfortunate fellow pathetically attempted to lap up a few drops with his tongue.

If the one whose feet have slipped had once been high and mighty, the subsequent contempt is even greater. In words that

sound like the other side of the *Magnificat,* Job laments the fall
of the chiefs. The Virgin Mary rejoiced that God "has put down
the mighty from their thrones, and exalted those of low degree."
Job says the same thing, only he does not rejoice over it. "He
leads counselors away stripped, and judges he makes fools. He
looses the bonds of kings, and binds a waistcloth on their loins.
He leads priests away stripped, and overthrows the mighty. . . .
He takes away understanding from the chiefs of the people of
the earth, and makes them wander in the pathless wastes."

Job undoubtedly is thinking of himself as he describes the
chiefs whom God has made to "grope in the dark without
light." The contrast between the social prestige that he once
had and the social rejection that he now knows is the bitter pill
he has to swallow. In his humiliation he is supersensitive to
Zophar's arrogance. Because he was of the ruling class, he could
never exalt over their collapse. Yet those of low degree may find
devious delight in the fall of the mighty as a reaction to the
obeisance that they have felt compelled to extend. When these
high ones have fallen, the low ones may seize the opportunity
to retaliate. The hatred that now may savagely be released had
been stored up behind the servility that was demanded of them
by their lowly niche in the societal structure. Here is the wisdom
implicit in the proverb, "Never make a slave a king."

Rather than quarrel over Zophar's insistence upon the sovereignty of God, Job takes the offensive by asking who would
ever doubt it. Even the animal kingdom, the beasts, birds, fish,
yes, even the plant kingdom acknowledge it. The problem is that
such sovereignty is of no comfort to him now. Of *course* it is
the hand of the Lord that has afflicted him. But this only
aggravates the problem by provoking questions from Job that
he would not have previously asked. Since his friends are where
he used to be, their words are judged by his ears as stale food

is judged by the tongue. Job has experienced the movement of history. New situations bring forth new questions. The new questions hopefully lead to new answers. In this way our movement in time becomes progress. Yet the time gap between the eruption of the questions and the arrival of the answers can be an agonizing interval.

Job is questioning the very formulas by which he once had structured his life. The Job whose eyes are opened is rebelling against the Job who used to be. What his friends know he also knows. The old Job believed these arguments as much as they. The answers are simple when one does not have the problem. But when he *has* the problem, he raises questions that his previous frame of reference would not have recognized. He faces existentially hitherto unrealized complications. No wonder Job is furious when his friends try to answer these complications with the old formulas.

What could his counselors offer him that would actually be of help? Can they take away his boils? This would certainly help. Can they bring back his children from the dead? How often we wish we could restore the lost for the bereaved. Can they reestablish his social status? Are not these his losses and their restoration his answer? Yet they can offer him none of these things. They are in the same position the pastor is in today when he ministers to those similarly afflicted.

What other can the pastor give who cannot give the restoration of the lost? He can offer the sufferer the support of his own person. He can close ranks behind him. He represents the solidarity of the congregation which is upholding the sufferer with its compassion and prayers. His offer is essentially what God offers—a sustaining relationship in which to work out his answers.

To the three friends as well as to present-day comforters, the simple offer of their relationship seems woefully inadequate.

Since they cannot restore the lost, they resort to giving advice. This they feel is at least *something* that they can give to justify their presence. It is precisely at this point that they disclose their *own* needs. They feel inadequate as *persons*. Yet it is our person that the sufferer desires. For the comforter to minimize or even to disparage the giving of his person is to show his ignorance of what *ministry* actually is. Job might have realized the divine relationship if the comforters had given to him its human reflection in their own persons. Though his anger at their failure proved to be a strengthening factor, he might have experienced the revelation of God much sooner if his comforters had communicated empathy rather than judgment.

It is not uncommon for a person in reflecting upon his period of affliction to be grateful especially for the support of friends. In these times of trial the fellowship of believers can become a living experience. The analogy of the church to the human body becomes meaningful when one knows the other members of the Body are feeling with him in his affliction. This tangible demonstration of *care* cuts into the natural isolating effects of sickness and bereavement. Its therapeutic influence begins at this point.

Job grew weary of arguing with those who had no basis in experience for understanding his problem. "What you know, I also know." Instead he desires to "argue his case with God." He evaluates the counseling of his friends as worthless. "Worthless physicians all of you!" They have done nothing but "whitewash with lies." Their "comfort" is so galling to him that he longs for the good old days when they ministered to him in silence for seven days and seven nights. In fact, he suggests they return to them. "Oh that you would keep silent, and it would be your wisdom!"

Job's major complaint against his friends is that they have

whitewashed God. He attacks them for defending God—for trying to take God "off the hook." Not only is such partiality unfair, but God himself is against it. "He will surely rebuke you," warns Job, "if in secret you show partiality." Pleading the case for God is a typical pastoral pitfall. Therefore we need to hear it straight from Job that God neither needs such partiality nor does he want it. When we become God's public-relations men, we, like the three friends, are really grinding our own axes. In playing down his dubious qualities and playing up his good qualities, we think we are doing God a service, but actually such tactics reveal our own doubts about God's ways. Our defenses, says Job, are defenses of clay, and in consequence the dread of God should fall upon us.

Since the three friends have each accused him in turn of having no dread of God because of his outspoken, albeit honest complaint, Job turns the tables on them and accuses them of having no dread of God for their traditional, albeit dishonest defense. The use of the half-truth to cover over the whole truth is a distortion of the truth. To speak deceitfully for God is to invite upon oneself the terror of God's majesty. To the three friends, God represents the order, meaning, and structure to life. Shake the foundation and the whole structure is shaken. Their defense of God is their attempt to keep this structure intact. Behind their defense is the fear that the structure may collapse under Job's attack. Therefore they must attack Job to prevent this from happening.

3. JOB'S DESPERATE PIONEERING

Having dispensed with his comforters as incompetent, Job turns his attention to God. As with his friends so with God he decides to give complete abandonment to his feelings. This is a risk that many of us rarely if ever take. Ours is a comformist age and we are reluctant to permit our honesty to endanger our relationships. We fear to make an enemy—especially when he is a very important personage—such as God. Yet Job is desperate enough to take the risk. He will take his flesh in his teeth—put his life in his hands—and do it with his eyes open. Though God may slay him, he still will not back down, for he is determined to "defend my ways to his face."

Job is indirectly revealing his confidence in God. Behind his attacks upon God's character there is the ambivalent confidence in his grace. With one breath he says God may slay him, and with another he voices hope in God's acceptance. He knows he has a good case, and therefore he knows he shall be vindicated. But there are certain conditions that must prevail for such an encounter. Once again Job asks God to dispense with his wrathful side. In spite of his determination not to quaver, Job has second thoughts. The dread of God will surely terrify him unless God withdraws his retaliating hand.

It seems to the sufferer that God counts him as an enemy. "Wilt thou frighten a driven leaf and pursue dry chaff?" In requesting God to put aside his wrath, Job is in reality asking again for a mediator—an umpire. It is not without significance that Christ in his sufferings endured this same agony of rejection. From the cross came the cry, "My God, my God, why hast thou forsaken me?" Yet how can Christ be the mediatorial God-man and still be forsaken by God? Actually it is in the experience of forsakenness that he becomes the mediator. His identification with man had to encompass the nadir of human experience, and his identification with God had to reckon with God's wrath. Here was the "expiating self-sacrifice offered up to the wrath of God's dark side," as Jung puts it.[1]

[1] *Answer to Job*, p. 155.

Yet the value of Christ's mediation through identification may not be existentially perceived in the moment of despair. In his *Letters to Malcolm,* C. S. Lewis attempted to comfort his bereaved friend by elucidating on the fact that Christ also protested against God's apparent rejection. Yet in his own subsequent grief, Lewis found this of little comfort. "C reminded me," he writes, "that the same thing seems to have happened to Christ: 'Why hast thou forsaken me?' I know. Does that make it easier to understand?"

Like Lewis, Job had to work out his own answers. In his searching he came to the conclusion that he must be suffering for the iniquities of his youth. Most of us have acted out enough youthful impulses to be able to resurrect some hidden guilt. In the painful process of coming into his own identity as an adult, the adolescent has an affinity for feeling guilty. He learns how to hide it and finally how to grow out of it. Unfortunately, however, he may not always have resolved it. It lurks instead in the forgotten corners of the misty past until the anxieties from some future trauma such as Job's calamity draw it back to light. "The chickens," we say, "have come home to roost." Perhaps the guilt needs the calamity as much as the calamity needs the guilt. In our orientation to a guilt and punishment sequence, the sins of our youth remain hidden in the wings until the ominous cues signal their entrance onto the stage.

But this is to make much ado about so little. Man himself is so insignificant, let alone the sins of his long past youth. He wastes away like a garment that is moth-eaten. Job uses the familiar biblical figure of man's transitory nature—the flower. He blooms for a time and then withers away. By what heavenly logic, then, can God bring such a fragile and transient piece of creation into judgment? "Dost thou open thy eyes upon such a one?" Why am I being singled out? While some may long for even negative attention as an alternative to no attention, Job prefers to be ignored. If he is a sinner, he is also a helpless sinner. "Who can bring a clean thing out of an unclean?" In his despair, Job sees only the determined side of human existence: freedom is an ironic myth. Since you have appointed my bounds, God, that I cannot pass, why don't you leave me without responsibility like a hireling instead of making demands upon me as though I were the one in charge? If this is what it means to be a son, Job prefers to be the hired man.

Since the past is over and the present is intolerable, Job turns his eyes to the future. For a person who feels as isolated as he, the Hebrew view of life after death was exasperatingly vague. The only certainty was death. What lay beyond for the individual believer was nebulous and shadowy. The word was *Sheol*—the land of shades and shadows and semi-conscious existence. In the face of such subliminal haze, Job dared to raise the question of hope. The situation is the reverse of today when we have in our theological tradition positive statements and even descriptions about life after death. In our disturbances, we dare to raise the question of *no* hope. Life for the Hebrew of Job's day was communal and religion was a group experience. How then could he think clearly about the survival of the individual?

Also, in Hebrew thinking a person was a body-soul being. In death the body obviously ceases to function and deteriorates to dust. How then could one take his body into any life after death? If there were no body, how could there still be a person? For the neighboring Greeks to the west and Asians to the east this was no problem. In contrast to the Hebrews, these cultures thought of the body as a hindrance to the soul rather than an expression of it. Hence to slough off the body at death created no conflict for a belief in eternal life. In fact, it made such a belief possible. The soul was finally emancipated from its prison. In contrast, the Hebrews had a doctrine of creation: the body was good and nature was God's handiwork. Consequently, Job sees more survival hope for a tree than for man. If a tree is cut down, new shoots come up from the dead stump. Yet when a man dies and is laid low, where is he? He certainly will not rise again as the new shoot. "Till the heavens are no more he will not awake."

But Job cannot leave it there. His feelings for God move him also to hope. If he does not receive his satisfaction in this life, he hopes that somehow it will yet come after death. "Oh that thou wouldest hide me in Sheol, . . . that thou wouldest appoint me a set time, and remember me!" His hope for eventual justice confronts him with the ultimate question: "If a man die, shall he live again?" If he could believe the answer were *yes,* he would willingly endure his sufferings as he awaited his eventual release. The very thought of this possibility affects him emotionally. Job is touched as his need for affection rises to the surface. "Thou wouldest call, and I would answer thee; thou wouldest long for the work of thy hands."

Caught up in his hope for eventual restoration, Job for the moment seems to have achieved his peace. He speaks as though his hope were already fulfilled. But the former despair is too deeply embedded to allow his feelings to soar for long. They soon crash as his habitual doubting returns with his cultural conception of eternity. He descends into utter desolation and despair. "But the mountain falls and crumbles away, . . . so thou destroyest the hope of man." So high the hope, so low the depression. In contrast to the anticipation of intimacy with which he was momentarily absorbed, Job sees only the stark reality of his emptiness and isolation. Yet man must hope. Along with faith and love, hope shall abide. Job's despair also will not remain unchallenged.

4. ELIPHAZ' RECURRENT THEME— JUSTICE WILL OUT

As Job's words end in despair, Eliphaz enters the fray for the second time. Although he is more biting in his criticism than before, the theme of his discourse is the same—justice will out. We still use the saying: "God's mill grinds slow but sure." In our day, however, we are released from the press of time under which Eliphaz chafed because we have the eternal dimension within which God can act. Will sinners be punished? If not in this life, we say, at least in the life beyond. Eliphaz in his eschatological uncertainty says that justice must be meted out in this life. Will the righteous be blessed? In Eliphaz' thinking, the blessing also has to come in life before death. If we understood the significance of the question, "Does Job fear God for nought?" as Job and his contemporaries understood it, we would have to dispense also with the eternal blessings promised to the faithful. The question therefore is comparable to that once asked of Calvinist ordinands: "Are you willing to be damned for the glory of God?"

Eliphaz shows a complete lack of understanding as he uses Job's catharsis as evidence to condemn him. "Your own mouth condemns you, and not I." Who do you think you are, Job, talking like this! "Do you limit wisdom to yourself? What do you know that we do not know?" How Job must have despaired when he heard this! His sufferings had brought him into a world of doubt that they had never experienced. Since they cannot recognize this simple fact, it is obvious that they can never understand. Instead of recognizing the therapy in Job's catharsis, Eliphaz asks him why he lets his heart carry him away. For Job to let such words go out of his mouth is the same as turning his spirit against God. The implication is that Job should repress his resentment rather than let "his eyes flash." Nor will he permit him to defend himself by saying that he is a sinner even as all men are sinners. It is true that none born of women can be clean. But what has this to do with one who "drinks iniquity like water"? Job is more than a sinner in general; he is a specific sinner. Just talking as he has is more than enough to condemn him. This in itself is his iniquity.

Eliphaz' logic is the same as that used by Caiaphas against Jesus. The high priest was having his troubles getting a case against Jesus because the accusing witnesses were in disagreement. Then he asked the accused to speak for himself. "You will see the Son of man sitting at the right hand of Power," said Jesus, "and coming with the clouds of heaven." Hearing this, Caiaphas tore his mantle, and said, "Why do we still need witnesses? You have heard his blasphemy" (Mark 14:62-64). "Your own lips testify against you," said Eliphaz. Now we have you!

Eliphaz will not face the facts in Job's argument because they are too threatening. Since the recompense for evil and the reward for good have to be in this life, what about all the obvious exceptions? To Eliphaz, these exceptions are only transient illusions. To Job they are mocking realities. Eliphaz chose to avoid the head-on encounter by hammering instead on the principle that God punishes the evil and rewards the good. This is an example of the dishonesty in a half-truth defense of God's ways with men. Because they see only what they want to see, God's defenders can become demonic in the extremes to which they may go in preserving the half-true structure of their little world. The wicked man "will be paid in full before his time, and his branch will not be green." By affirming this again and again, the comforters think to fix its unalterability. At least it helps them to believe it.

5. JOB FIXES RESPONSIBILITY WITH GOD

Job sees the anxiety behind Eliphaz' defense. What is threatening you? What is the red flag that sets you off? "What provokes you that you answer?" Job sees even further. "If you were in my place I also could speak as you." Reverse the roles and place Eliphaz in Job's plight, and Job knows that he would "shake his head at him" as Eliphaz is now doing to Job. Instead of "joining words together against him" in judgment, however, he realizes now what the role of the comforter should be. He could strengthen the afflicted with his mouth and assuage his pain with the solace of his lips. This insight into the purpose of pastoral care came from the sufferer's own experience of need.

His reference to the assuaging of pain reminded Job that his own pain was not assuaged. Although Eliphaz had condemned him for expressing his resentment over this pain, Job is in no mood to defend himself. "If I speak, my pain is not assuaged, and if I forbear, how much of it leaves me?" Whether I speak out or repress, nothing helps. I am beat. Who is to blame? "Surely now God has worn me out." Job holds God responsible for all his troubles—even those with his friends. It is God who has the power, not they. There is an analogy in the way that the United States has learned through experience to hold Russia responsible for whatever trouble her satellites cause us. More often the reverse is true. The sufferer may be really angry with God but is afraid to say so and displaces his anger onto others. At least Job has the courage to quarrel with God directly. He charges him with injustice in the most grisly of images. "He slashes open my kidneys, and does not spare; he pours out my gall on the ground."

It is all so undeserved! Job's eyes are red with weeping although there is no violence in his hands and his prayer is pure. Even

71

though he has been abused by God, he has not been vindictive in return. Job has developed a good case of feeling sorry for himself—the victim of an outrageous piece of injustice. He appeals to the universe not to let his grievance be forgotten. "O earth, cover not my blood, and let my cry find no resting place." Do not let my protest pass away, for such would only add to the meaninglessness of life. For the sake of meaning, the outrage must be recognized!

As Job descends once more to the abyss of despair, the hope returns. Again it is the hope for a mediator. "Even now," he says, "my witness is in heaven, and he that vouches for me is on high." Although his friends scorn him, his hope is that God will maintain his right—that the mediator will defend him as a man would defend his neighbor. Job longs for this man-God type of intercessor because he feels so keenly how limited he is in his human body to reach the divine Spirit. Also the time for the body is short and the grave is readied. His defender must carry the cause even though Job will be no more.

Having given full vent to his attack on God, Job's confidence in God begins to prevail. God is responsible for his trouble—make no mistake about that! It is God who has even closed the minds of his friends. But by this same token Job believes he will not let them triumph over him. This is the other side of holding God responsible. Job believes that God will vindicate himself. Behind his attacks on God's justice is his confidence in God's integrity. Job believes in a moral universe in spite of the glaring evidence to the contrary rather than by denying these contradictions. Though his eyes have grown dim because of his weeping, he is not defeated. "He that has clean hands grows stronger and stronger." He will take his "comforters" on again. "But you, come on again, all of you, and I shall not find a wise man among you."

Job is under no illusions in his confidence. His goals, desires, ambitions, and plans are all broken off. Rather he has to live in the night. At this point he sounds like a negative St. Francis of Assisi. Where St. Francis identifies himself with nature, calling the earth his mother and the sun his brother, Job identifies himself with the negative elements of the dark world. If Sheol is his house and the Pit is his father and the worm is his mother or sister, where then is his hope? Whatever hope there is will come in the absence of all hope. There certainly is nothing to which the three friends can point in the tangible universe that can add any positive note to his miserable state.

6. BILDAD'S SECOND DISCOURSE

Bildad could scarcely be expected to let such a charge go unchallenged. Job's offensiveness brings a sarcastic counterattack. Are you so important, Job, that the universe has to adjust to you? "Why are we stupid in your sight? You who tear yourself in your anger, shall the earth be forsaken for you?" Yet after this initial invective Bildad can do no more than repeat the old refrain in more biting terms. The wicked will come to nought and Job had better wise up to the fact. The dialogue has now become a fight, and each attempts to subdue the other by sledging still more.

7. JOB CRIES FOUL!

Job comes back in kind. Even if it be true that he has erred, what business is it of theirs? His guilt is his own concern. Job deeply resents their attempt to make his humiliation an argument against him—an argument in which he is doomed from the start. Yet it is not an uncommon way of approaching those who are afflicted. Because their presence upsets our applecart, we may subconsciously resent them. When they are repulsive to us, we may desire to remove ourselves from their presence. Since the afflicted are the opposite of the beautiful, our feelings of attraction may change to repugnance. We may prefer that the afflicted did not exist, but since they do, we must do something about the pity they arouse—for it makes us anxious.

In like manner, we point to the fall of the mighty as judgment. See, he is fallen. Therefore he must in some way be responsible for it. *Ergo,* he deserved to fall. Now we are relieved from the responsibility of feeling sorry for him and becoming anxious over it. We can keep our anxiety down if we can believe that the afflicted one is reaping what he sowed. Even the tragedy of the cross could be reduced by this approach. To a large extent Christ brought his trouble on himself. He was his own worst enemy. He needlessly antagonized the Pharisees by calling them vile names in public. Obviously he could have handled the situation more diplomatically. By failing to do this, he made his presence intolerable to his enemies. Too bad—but what could he expect? In ways such as this, we perpetuate the ancient belief that our sufferings are in proportion to our sins. The negative must be accounted for as a judgment for the sake of justice and the meaningfulness of life.

To all this Job cries *foul!* As a victim of this argument in a circle, his own sense of justice is outraged. "I know," he insists, "that God has put me in the wrong, and closed his net about me. Behold, I cry out 'Violence!' but I am not answered; I call aloud, but there is no justice." He feels trapped by an arbitrary God who has "walled up his way" and "set darkness upon his paths." He feels stripped by this same fate from any glory that he once may have had. Job knows the contrast—the crown was on his head—and so the stripping hurts all the more. He has

74

been deposed from his position of prominence and estranged from the circle of his intimates—and it is God who has done it! There is no need on Job's part to protect God so that God will protect him. He feels no compunction to blame people when it is God who has the power.

It is a humiliating reversal in status when the servant is beseeched by his former master. It is even more humiliating when even then the servant refuses to answer. What pride is left to one when he is repulsive to his own wife and loathsome to his own brothers, when those whom he loves, his intimates, have turned against him? Despite all the deservedly fine things we say about children, they can be very cruel to those more helpless. In a culture where age was respected, the show of disrespect from children was the last straw in Job's broken self-respect. He paints his picture of rejection so movingly that he himself is overcome by it. He breaks down and pleads once more for compassion. "Have pity on me, have pity on me, O you my friends, for the hand of God has touched me!" With no pride left to him, Job reaches out pathetically for rapport and begs his comforters not to be like God. "Why do you, like God, pursue me? Why are you not satisfied with my flesh?"

Out of the deepest despair comes the highest hope. The way up may be down. Job again hits the depths and rises to the heights. "Oh that my words were written! . . . that with an iron pen and lead they were graven in the rock for ever!" With these words, Job begins his great profession of faith. "For I know that my Redeemer lives, and at last he will stand upon the earth; and after my skin has been thus destroyed, then without [or: from] my flesh I shall see God." Here is an eschatological faith that overcomes both the problems of individuality and of the physical body. As a person—as an individual—he shall see God! In spite of his lack of cultural support and the obvious disintegration of a corpse, Job believes that God will vindicate him, and that he shall witness it. Such a faith was not easy to maintain in the fluctuation of his moods. Therefore he wants to tack it down —hold it—grave it in rock, as a testimony to himself and to posterity.

In his renewed confidence, Job sees the coming judgment upon his friends. His faith is in God's integrity and not in theirs. In seeking to blame him for his troubles, they are inviting the wrath of the sword upon them.

8. ZOPHAR REENTERS THE FRAY

Zophar reacts to Job's warning with increasing antagonism. But his argument—like Bildad's—is like a broken record. The wicked may exalt, but only for a short time, and the joy of the godless is but for a moment. Though his bones are full of youthful vigor, it will lie down with him in the dust. Though he swallows riches, he will vomit them up again. There is no escape, for this is the heritage that God has decreed for him.

The three friends seem never to progress in their thinking. In contrast to Job they are defending rather than digging and searching. So they simply repeat in more virulent language and more violent imagery the same old argument that the prosperity of the wicked that Job keeps shoving in their faces has the seeds within it of its own destruction.

Yet healing is taking place nevertheless. The three friends are at least talking with Job at the level of his feelings and needs, even if argumentatively. This is more therapeutic than were they to clam up, change the subject, or withdraw, leaving the sufferer with his ailing spirit to the ravages of infection. They are sharing, however defensively, in the area where Job is thinking and feeling, and catharsis, however violent, is taking place.

VII

JOB'S DEFIANT TRIUMPH

Job 21–31

When Zophar began his second discourse by saying, "I hear
censure which insults me," he indicated the level to which they
all had now adapted in their dialogues. Job reflected this same
antagonism when he reacted to Zophar by asking that he listen
to what he has to say and then "mock on." Job still has points he
wants to press. The first of these is his physical appearance.
"Look at me," he demands, "and be appalled." The ravages of
his disease had left him hideous.

1. LOOK AT ME

"Look at me!" This is precisely what we comforters find difficult to do. We prefer to look away or even to ignore. The forgotten people in our veterans hospitals and rest homes are the
evidence of our neglect. The elderly particularly bear the brunt
of our tendency to look away. I know of one aged man whose
grandchildren are "excused" from visiting him because of his
offensive physical disabilities. Even as I am writing this en route
by train I discovered myself hoping that a physically deformed
person who had just boarded would choose some other seat than
beside me. Realizing that I felt this way, I automatically cen-

77

sured myself and even hoped that this individual would sit by me and relieve my guilt. Yet none of this subsequent compensation can eliminate my initial reaction. As Job says, "Be appalled if you will, but continue to look."

We see the opposite tendency in Jesus. He shocked his contemporaries by actually touching the unclean lepers. A student chaplain in a cancer hospital was concerned about how he would react to his patients. He was afraid he might want to look away. He discovered, however, that after he involved himself in a ministry to these patients he became less aware of their physical symptoms. Those who have the courage to look lose their discomfort even though they initially may "lay their hands upon their mouths."

2. BOLD DENIAL OF THE CAUSE-AND-EFFECT FORMULA

Having made his point about his physical appearance, Job denies Zophar's argument. The world is full of incongruities and injustices of which the sight of Job is a prime example. The children of the wicked are established in their presence and their houses are safe from fear. In contrast Job is bereft of all his children and his house has collapsed. The bull breeds for the wicked and the cow calves, but Job's flocks and herds have been destroyed.

Few religious people express their disillusion as boldly as Job, and yet their actions at times may indicate the same sentiment. "What is the Almighty, that we should serve him? And what profit do we get if we pray to him?" This question takes us back to the prologue with its question, "Does Job fear God for nought?" This profit motive is just as pertinent a reason for *not* fearing God as for fearing him. Is it not the wicked who are prosperous? Today we say it differently. The rich, we say, can do anything. If he has enough money, he can hire the best image builders and get himself elected to office and even control the press. Although the role played by the Kennedy fortune in the Kennedy political campaigns has given impetus to this belief, it did not create it. The tycoons are known more for their power than for their ethics. Add money to organizational mastery and administrative rigging—and empires, political, economic, religious, can be built. The fact that the sons of the tycoons become respectable and law-abiding only adds fuel to Job's fire. Why are these sins of the past swept under the rug and the profit from them allowed to remain?

Job and his friends were well aware that the rewards as well as the judgments of God are not all settled in one generation. Rather these retributions were carried out to third and fourth generation. Yet Job will not allow his friends this recourse. What evidence of justice is it if God stores up their iniquity for their sons? Let him recompense it to *them*. "Let their own eyes see their destruction." Only in this way can justice be said to exist.

We also take recourse in the future, only we extend the period for retribution into eternity. This obscures the issue even more since the third and fourth generations were at least potentially observable. Even as Job saw the injustice in punishing posterity for the sins of the fathers, so by implication he would resist the unverifiable nature of any recourse to eternity. The man in the street has repeatedly resented the way official religion postpones to eternity the advantages he desires. I recall an incident from the depression of the thirties that illustrates this resentment. As I awaited my turn in the cut-rate barber shop, the men around me were expressing the futility of those days. One of them with tongue in cheek noted that his preacher had said things would be better in heaven. The disgusted retort of the barber stuck in my young mind. "I want my heaven now," he said, "not after I'm dead." This has been the communist appeal to any deprived people and its criticism of official religion. The oppressed want their deliverance now. Negroes want their civil rights *now*. The poor want jobs *now*. Promises for tomorrow only infuriate. *Now* is the only time consonant with reality.

The postponing of retribution to posterity is music to the wicked's ears. "For what do they care for their houses after them?" We have examples of this attitude from the Old Testament itself. When Hezekiah the King foolishly showed the storehouses of Judah to Babylonian emissaries, Isaiah the prophet warned him that the day was coming when all that was in those storehouses would be carried away into Babylon. Even good King Hezekiah accepted the warning without great concern. "Why not," he reasoned, "if there will be peace and security in my days?" Again when Elijah the prophet warned Ahab, king of Israel, about the dire consequences of the murder of Naboth, the king put on sackcloth and ashes and fasted in repentance. Because of his penitent attitude, the judgment was changed. The evil would not come in his days but in his son's days.

So where is the difference between what happens to the wicked and the good? There is none! One who is evil may live a full life in prosperity and one who is righteous may die in bitterness without having ever tasted the good. Only in death is there any universality. "They lie down alike in the dust, and the worms cover them." How then can you speak about the justice of God? The more Job suffered, the more isolated he felt. The elation associated with community experience was gone. Alone in his sickness, he has become preoccupied with his negative uniqueness. Estranged from others by his affliction, he is concerned about what happens to the individual sufferer—to himself.

From this perspective he sees nothing but inequity and an almost devious deprivation of justice. Nor is he alone in this observation. Ask those who travel the roads—the caravaners of the East. In contrast to the three friends, they know life beyond the parochial boundaries. They will tell you the same as Job—that the wicked man is spared in the day of calamity. Who brings the prince to account? Who confronts the wicked to his face? Job's questions are hard to evade. Even in death the wicked is treated preferentially. A watch is kept over his tomb. We are reminded of the carefully guarded tomb of Lenin where even the body of the communist leader is remarkably preserved. In the face of these obvious discrepancies, Job chides Zophar for confronting him with empty nothings. You are simply not honest. There is nothing left of your answers but falsehood.

Having scathingly exposed the half-truths in his comforters' arguments, Job has made a shambles of their rational system. He has so forcefully put forth his evidence against the justice of God that he leaves one with the impression that he has now heard the opposite half-truth. Is life really as devoid of pattern as the sufferer sees it? Or is he also prone to oversimplify things?

3. ELIPHAZ' VICIOUS ATTACK

When one can no longer attack the arguments of his opponent, he may attack his person. The very violence with which Job shattered the position of his comforters brought forth from Eliphaz a vicious attack upon Job's character. Does Job really think he is having an effect on God with all his charges when it is so obvious that it is because of his wickedness that God is entering into judgment with him? Gone are those innuendos and veiled accusations; the attack is direct and unmitigated. "Is not your wickedness great and your iniquities endless?" Job himself is now the wicked tycoon upon whom justice has come. Eliphaz accuses him of stripping the clothing of the naked, withholding water from the weary and bread from the hungry, sending widows away empty, and breaking orphans' arms. Not only is the attack direct, it is also without foundation. The wildness of Eliphaz' accusations is the mark of his desperation.

Yet he holds out hope. There is still time for Job to yield—to submit—so that good can come to him. He pictures this good in as extreme a manner as he indicted Job's character. Not only will God receive Job if he changes his attitude, but he will even deliver others who are not innocent by Job's clean hands. For coming into line the reward will be great. God will exalt Job to the position of a confidant who can intercede for others. Job's longing for such an intercessor for himself will be transcended by his own appointment to this role for others.

4. THE HIDDEN GOD

Eliphaz' attack was so vicious that Job evidently felt it useless even to attempt refutation. Realizing the futility of arguing his case before his comforters, he directs his attention to God. "Oh, that I knew where I might find him, that I might come even to his seat! I would lay my case before him." Job longed for understanding into the mystery of his calamity. He wanted to know how God would defend himself against his accusations. First he feared that God would attack him for his audacity; then he believed that God would listen sympathetically and justice would be restored.

Of what value, however, are such musings when God is nowhere to be found? Though he looks forward and backward and to the right and to the left, he cannot perceive him. Yet he is convinced that God sees *him*. This conviction restores him to hope. Thus the inner wheels of his mind never stop turning as he vacillates from hope to despair. At times he gets an insight into a possible purpose to his ordeal. "When he tests me, I shall emerge as gold." At other times he lapses back into anguished frustration. "He is unchangeable and who can turn him? What he wishes, that he does." Who can be more irascible to approach than a hidden God whose activities are arbitrary if not whimsical? There is no lever that man can use to move him—no wedge that he can drive into his infuriating self-sufficiency. Not even Job's integrity can influence him. God is unmoved by Job's righteousness.

5. THE HARDENED GOD

But is God unmoved by Job's defiance? Job feels unsure of his ground at this point. "God has made my heart weak." He contemplates the terror of God and wishes to vanish in darkness. The fear that he may have gone too far in antagonizing God sends him scurrying for cover. One cannot fight *God!* Yet why can God not keep times of court like any other ruler? Why can he not be like a man! Evil and injustice are running rampant and God either does not know or does not care. At least he is doing nothing to stop it. Those who are on top are the lowest of people. They take the widow's ox for a pledge and snatch the fatherless child from the breast.

In his fall down the social ladder Job has developed a strong identification with the underdog. He feels with the poor of the earth who are thrust off the road by those in control. His calamity has created an authority problem for him. By what right does one lord it over another? By what possible logic does God exercise *his* authority? When the groans of the dying and the cries for help of the wounded come to his ears, what does he do? Nothing! He pays no attention to their prayer. The result of this calloused disregard of God's for the afflicted of the earth is that the murderer and adulterer and all other powers of darkness are having a heyday.

Job anticipates how his friends will attempt to refute his indictment of God. They will say that the prosperity of the wicked is but for a short time. This to Job is a blatant refusal to face the facts. God actually prolongs the life of the wicked exploiter of the poor. If such is not so, let them prove him wrong. He challenges them to present the evidence.

6. MAINTAINING HIS INTEGRITY

Instead of responding to the challenge, Bildad resorts again to intimidation. Who is Job to talk this way about God? If even the stars are not clean in his sight, how can a mortal man—who is in comparison a mere worm—appeal to his own righteousness? Bildad has touched a raw nerve in that Job has known his moments of dread. There were those times, as we have seen, when he was tempted to surrender his defiance for fear of the divine terror. Bildad's appeal to his temptation forces Job to deal directly with it. Despite the frightening aspect of carrying on a solitary fight against God, Job cannot yield. To do so would be to sell his soul for a mess of safety. As God lives, he will not speak falsehood. Were he to give in because of his dread of the Almighty, he would be sacrificing his integrity. "Till I die," he vows, "I will not put away my integrity from me."

His conviction of his own righteousness is all that he has left. To deny it for the sake of peace would be to lose the one asset that he still retains—his self-respect. "Far be it from me to say that you are right. . . . My heart does not reproach me for any of my days." Because Job has the courage to hold out against the threats and bribes of his comforters, he is driven to maintain his integrity with an exaggerated affirmation. He has no regrets over any of his ways—none whatever! This overstatement of his innocence is his defiant reaction to the attempts of his friends to put him on the defensive. It is his offensive defense.

Zophar's third speech is missing. In all probability it is only the words, "And Zophar said," that are missing. Although chapter 27 is attributed to Job, vss. 13-23 sound like Zophar. In the balance and symmetry of the poem Zophar would seemingly have a third speech like the others. Assuming that 27:13-23 is the third speech of Zophar, he has "shot his wad." Having no intention to talk to the issues which Job has repeatedly raised, he merely repeats his old "dodge." The portion of the wicked man is bad, bad, bad. "The east wind lifts him up and he is gone." But the evidence Job asked for is not forthcoming. The dialogues have hit a stalemate.

Chapter 28 is an ode to wisdom that for unknown reasons has been inserted into the dialogues at this point, although it obviously is not a part of the dialogues. In Chapter 29 we take up the final speech of Job.

7. THE BITTER CONTRAST

With the present so odious and the future shrouded in darkness, Job's thoughts turn to the past as he recalls the "good old days." The pattern is similar to Psalm 77 in which the psalmist reflects upon the past to find the support from which present reverses have deprived him. "I consider the days of old," he says when his troubles overwhelm him. "I remember the years long ago." (v. 5.) So also Job says, "Oh, that I were as in the months of old, as in the days when God watched over me."

Yet his thoughts about the former days left him more bitter

than strengthened. The contrast was too painful. Although his description of his past is probably more glorious than it actually was—the past has a way of improving with age—he nevertheless had been a prominent figure in his community. When he took his place with the rulers at the gate, the young withdrew in respect, the aged rose and stood, and the princes refrained from talking. In his "autumn years" Job "sat as a chief." Why was he so respected? Because he delivered the poor who cried and the fatherless who had none to help him. Let Eliphaz take note! Behind Job's prestige was his concern for the deprived. He was eyes to the blind, feet to the lame, and a father to the poor. Why should he think otherwise than that he would die "in his nest, multiplying his days as the sand"? Would this indicate that Satan had been right about Job? Obviously he had anticipated only the continuance of God's blessings to the end of his days.

But now it all seems like a nightmare. His calamity had caught him off guard. Evidently the possibility of such a catastrophe had never entered his mind. Of all his troubles none is more bitter than his social fall. He before whom the aged stood now is sport to those younger than he, whose fathers he would not have entrusted with his dogs. He has become the song, the byword, of this senseless, disreputable brood of ne'er-do-wells whom society had driven from its midst. These dregs of the earth are now saying, "Aha!" to the fallen chief. Casting off all restraint they spit at the sight of this repulsive sufferer. Taking sadistic delight in this reversal of roles, they release upon him their chronic resentment. Such humiliation outrages Job's sensitivities.

And whom does Job hold responsible for all this? God! He is the adversary who has "loosed his cord and humbled him." If he could escape even momentarily from his anguish! Yet even at night the pain that gnaws him gives him no rest. For this also God is to blame. He has cast Job into the mire, and when

86

he cries out he gives no heed. "God has turned cruel to me." Though Job feels doomed, he still stretches out his hand for help.

Job insists he had not been indifferent toward those who were in the straits in which he now finds himself. "Did I not weep for him whose day was hard?" So how in any rational sense could he possibly be reaping what he sowed? It is all so unjust! "When I looked for good, evil came." In saying this Job indicates that he had shared the cause-and-effect formula of his friends. Because he was an upright man who had compassion on the poor, he anticipated that he would be prosperous and content to the end of his days. His calamity upset the applecart. His whole *Weltanschauung* had collapsed. No wonder he could not stand to hear the old formulas from his friends. Plagued by anxiety over the loss of his landmarks, Job's mind dwells continually on his problems. "My heart is in turmoil, and is never still."

8. JOB'S CATALOGUE OF HIS VIRTUES

In what is to be the final affirmation of his case Job turns the microscope on every conceivable area of his life. Chapter 31 is a catalogue of Job's virtues by Job. It is his complete rebuttal of Eliphaz' attack. Obviously he has been stinging from this attack although he has not replied to it. In every area which he examines, Job exonerates himself with argumentative embellishment. His virtue has been on trial throughout the dialogues. Consequently he is driven to a detailed and all-out scrutiny of it.

The first area for examination is his sexual life. How could he look upon a virgin with lust, he asks, when he has made a covenant with his eyes? His argument is that as a committed person he has no private world even in his thoughts. Since the God to whom he is covenanted sees all, he would have to face him for any indulgence of the flesh. Job's fear of such an encounter is his evidence of his sexual integrity. Like Joseph who resisted Potiphar's wife, he too would say, "How then can I do this great wickedness, and sin against God?" (Gen. 39:9.) Job extends the argument from the virgin to the married woman. "If my heart has been enticed to a woman, and I have lain in wait at my neighbor's door . . . that would be a heinous crime." In fact any duplicity—any walking with falsehood—is out of bounds to one who is covenanted.

Job turns his attention next to the way in which he has treated his servants. Again the argument is the same. If he had rejected the cause of any of his servants when they brought a complaint against him, "what shall I do when God rises up?" Yet there is more to it than this. He treated his servants fairly also because he believed in the basic equality of all men before God. "Did not he who made me in the womb make him?"

His dealings with the poor are in the same category. Not only is he clean of any sins of commission against the destitute, he is also clean of sins of omission. He has withheld nothing from them; in fact he has taken a fatherly interest in them. If he ever took advantage of the fatherless, he would have had to face the majesty of God—and of this he was in terror.

Though he had been a rich man, Job insists that he never put his trust in wealth. Nor was his gold something in which he rejoiced. To do so would mean being "false to God above."

The acid test is not how a man treats his servants or the poor but how he feels toward his enemies. In this area Job now scrutinizes his soul. "If I have rejoiced at the ruin of him that hated me"—or even hidden iniquity in my bosom because I was afraid of what people would think. . . . The sentence is left unfinished. Instead Job cries out, "Oh, that I had one to hear me! . . . Oh, that I had the indictment written by my adversary!" All his searching has failed to yield anything. He cannot discover the indictment, and yet he knows it must be there. If God would only spell it out he would carry it on his shoulder or bind it on as a crown. He would gladly give account to God for all his steps. "Like a prince I would approach him." Obviously he has not been humbled by his calamity. Rather he is defiant in the honest conviction of his own limited perspective. He will enter any conference with God—at least in this momentary mood—with his head high.

As if his audacious confidence were too much even for *him,* Job seems to have a second thought or perhaps an afterthought. He had neglected the area of his stewardship of the land. But he has nothing to fear here either. "If my land has cried out against me, and its furrows have wept together; if I have eaten its yield without payment, and caused the death of its tenants, let thorns grow instead of wheat, and foul weeds instead of barley." Thus the words of Job were ended.

Job closed his discourse in a fanfare of self-justification—the epitome of virtue. The listener's reaction was expressed well by one of my students who said, "This guy Job really irritates me." He could understand how Eliphaz, Bildad, and Zophar felt. He irritated them also. So they ceased to answer Job "because he was righteous in his own eyes." "What's the use?" they probably asked. "You can't make any impression on *him.* Why bother? We're just wasting our breath."

Yet this is what happens to a person when he is shown no understanding. He becomes unattractive in his personality and defensively distorted in his perspective. The consequence of not being loved may be that one becomes unlovable. Job's conversations had become heated arguments. He had quarreled with his old friends. Few of us quarrel gracefully, especially with our intimates. Who would like to hear a tape recording, for example, of his marital quarrels? We would be embarrassed by the way in which our accusations of the other were matched only by our justification of ourselves. The dynamics of the quarrel could be summed up by shouting, "I'm justified and I'll be damned if I'll back down. It is *you* who are at fault." The effect, of course, is immediate rebuttal and countercharge. While those who others say are saints will deny any such status, those who claim to be saints themselves will soon find that others will deny them this status.

Job has been literally driven up the wall in defense. His hair is on end. Yet he is vital and triumphant in his defiance. His one comfort, one possession, is his integrity. Regardless of how wrong he may be, Job really believes he is right!

VIII

THE COURAGE TO RESPOND

1. OPEN vs. REPRESSED HOSTILITY

Pastorally speaking, Job's three friends did not know how well off they were in having Job's resentment at the surface. When hostility is repressed, the pastoral task is much more difficult. Yet they would have liked nothing better than for Job to repress his resentment.

We can understand their desire only too well. A little resentment goes a long way—and they had more than a little. Things are much more pleasant at the surface when people keep their hostility hidden, and many of us are willing to settle for surface appearances. We are pulled as by gravity away from tension and toward the congenial.

Job's friends chose the familiar ways to move Job to repress his resentment. We know them well because we have tried them ourselves, especially with our children. But with Job they simply did not work. Instead they made him even more defiant. With many of us, however, these methods are quite successful.

In analyzing the neurotic personality of our time, Karen Horney believes that hostility is the basic and least acceptable of our destructive emotions. It is that over which we feel guilty and concerning which we have anxiety. In fact her concept of basic anxiety—feeling lonely and helpless in a hostile world—is interwoven with a basic hostility. Yet it is a repressed hostility.

The insight into the destructive nature of repressed hostility belongs not only to the analysts of human nature but also to the portrayers of it. Playwright Arthur Miller, for example, shows it at work in *After the Fall*. Miller's stage setting in this play is within the mind of a lawyer suffering from a middle-age crisis. The lawyer, Quentin, has had two failures in marriage and in his own estimation is also a failure as a person. Behind his marital problems lies the repressed hostility toward a mother who had overrated him at the expense of a father whom she had emasculated before his own eyes. But Quentin could not tolerate this resentment toward the mother he was supposed to love. As a consequence he hid it behind an attempt to live up to her expectations for him. The clue to its presence was his inability to grieve when his mother died.

Though unrecognized, the resentment was projected into his relationship to his wives. This projection came to light in a very dramatic way when he attempted to throttle Maggie, his second wife, only to discover that in his own mental imagery he was throttling his mother. The shock opened his eyes to the truth. He realized then that "the wish to kill is never killed." The hate is there. How now to face the future with any hope? The answer is in "doing the hardest thing of all—see your own hatred, and live!"

Moralistic pressures move us to create the facades which we grow to believe ourselves. They generate the neurotic symptom which is simply a distraction or an overcompensation. To an observer the neurotic is making a mountain out of a molehill because the observer does not recognize what is actually being communicated through the symptom. If he could, he would recognize its mountain size as an overcompensation for something else—something too threatening to face directly. Often this "something else" is our hostile impulses. This is particularly likely when our hostility is directed toward one for whom it cannot be countenanced.

Quentin's mother in *After the Fall* obviously thought too much of him for his conscience to tolerate his resentment toward her. Our hostility is most likely to be uncountenanced when it is directed toward our intimates. The husband who repeatedly insists "I love my wife" to the counselor, may be trying to deny his resentment toward her. His very need to convince is indicative of his doubts.

It is difficult also to countenance hostility toward God. He too is an intimate—our Father—but he is much more. He is our Maker, our Judge, and our Redeemer. We need his good will too much to endanger it by feelings of resentment. Should circumstances arouse such feelings, we may automatically repress them. Also our religious activities may serve as compensations to deny such resentment. As Paul Tillich observes, "Have you ever noticed how much hostility against God dwells in the depths of the good and honest people, in those who excel in works of charity, in piety and religious zeal?" [1]

Dependency is something that all of us experience and most of us resent. God is the all-sufficient One upon whom we are infinitely dependent. We may chafe under this dependency even though we accept it for our survival. To express our resentment may sound like blasphemy. This was the reaction of Job's three friends to Job's heated remarks about God's arbitrary ways. Job wanted to reduce his dependency by asserting his right to hold God to account.

[1] *The New Being* (New York: Scribner's, 1955), p. 20.

93

Usually when a person experiences hostility toward one for whom hostility cannot be countenanced, he projects it to some safe object other than the real offender. Instead of blaming God, for example, he could blame the doctor, the minister, the weather, or the church. Job refused to do this. The three friends provided a natural scapegoat upon which to displace his anger over his calamity. Yet Job insisted upon focusing his hostility directly upon God. They had been in covenant together—God and Job—and now Job felt betrayed. His anger is of the quality that is directed toward intimates—or former intimates. Although Job displayed courage in directing his hostility toward its proper object, could he also have been evading a more unpleasant issue —the issue raised by the prologue—does Job fear God for nought? The intensity with which he accused God of violating his role in the covenant may obscure Job's lurking doubts about the quality of his own role in that covenant. Perhaps his heated attempts to establish his innocence before his three friends and God were also attempts to reassure himself.

2. DEFENSE AGAINST RECOGNIZING HOSTILITY

Those who differ from Job in that they cannot express their hostility may develop rigid defense systems to keep it from bursting like an unannounced child into open display. Yet they are always anxious lest its presence be detected nevertheless. Even when the hostility is largely unconscious—and it is never wholly unconscious—the anxiety over its exposure persists. However, such persons may not be aware of why they are anxious. Consequently they may need continual reassurance, often through expressions of affection, that their relationships are still intact. Such persons cannot tolerate the isolation of estrangement as could Job. All may be sacrificed—even honesty and self-respect—to keep their personal ties.

Job on the other hand valued his integrity more. In spite of his desperate need for help, he risked being cut off by man and God in his defiant refusal to give up his stand in order to be loved again. He had everything to gain by such a surrender and nothing to lose—but his honesty.

Those whose iniquity remains hidden have a need to maintain control of the punishment they feel they deserve. The very *hiddenness* of hostility adds to the sense of guilt. They have a need, therefore, for self-recrimination. Religiously speaking, they are cross-stealers. Their consciences are under the law and demand atonement, and the *hiddenness* of their guilt is an insuperable obstacle to any atonement by a mediator. By erecting their own cross they can retain control of the atoning process. The fear, whether recognized or not, is that this control might be lost and they would fall into the hands of the living God.

What one tries to accomplish by atonement, on the religious level, he attempts to achieve by overcompensation on the social scene. The strategy of overcompensation is that the hidden will remain hidden if one gives his neighbor the opposite impression. If he smiles, his neighbor is disarmed; he would never guess that behind the smile is an uncountenanced resentment. The more overtly friendly one is, the less likely his unfriendly thoughts will be discerned. His ties, therefore, can remain intact in spite of his hostility.

While overcompensation may maintain the surface aspects of a relationship, it obviously is a block to any sharing on the deeper levels. It is precisely such sharing that the overcompensator is attempting to avoid. Job's relationships were openly hostile and for this reason could not be considered superficial. The same can be said for his relationship with God. He was angry with God and made no attempt to hide it. Since he is one of the "saints" in the biblical tradition, his example can be helpful in the pastoral ministry to the afflicted whose piety will not permit the expression of their true feelings.

A hospital chaplain was concerned about a middle-aged house-wife with a terminal cancer because her religious faith made it impossible for her to face her real feelings about her condition. "I must not blame God," she said. "That would be wrong." Knowing her respect for the authority of the Bible, the pastor asked, "Have you thought about Job during these days?"

"As a matter of fact I have," she replied. "Job blamed God, didn't he?" asked the chaplain. She paused, taken back a bit, and then said, "But I just don't feel that way. I really *don't* blame God."

The chaplain accepted her position and let the matter rest. During his ministry to her a few days later, she said, "I just can't understand why God is putting me through all this." She was beginning to permit herself to look at her ambivalent feelings. The pastor's ministry had communicated to her that he would be acceptive if she expressed a negative sentiment. But it was Job who supported his witness that God also would be acceptive. Once a confrontation between her acceptable and unacceptable feelings was permitted, it was only a matter of time before her habitual resistance to such a confrontation would cease. The pastor had used Job to cut through the *should* to reach the *is*. He assisted the patient in the name of the authoritative Word to overcome her religious resistance to acknowledging and accepting reality.

There is a certain daring that accompanies the expression of anger. One is risking alienation for honesty of expression. When his father reprimanded him in anger, a small boy said, "You must hate me!" Because we know our anger can give this impression, we may hold back. We do not wish to alienate anyone. If by being genuine in our communication we may threaten our ties, our tendency is to be less than genuine. This Job refused to do. He chose his integrity above the security of his relationships. Because of this, he was deemed offensive, even blasphemous, by his friends.

Job's opposite is the person who keeps his anger to himself or even represses it from consciousness. In Luther's words, he is one who cannot "sin bravely." In my experience, the pastor is more likely to minister to this person than to one like Job. Most of us have consciences that are "under the law." We are in bondage to the fear of retribution—of abandonment—of being swallowed up by non-being. The tryannical conscience keeps a boundary between one's public or even conscious self and his angry, hostile self. Salvation in this case seems dependent upon keeping the two selves apart.

The good news of God's salvation in Christ applies, however, to the total person. It is the angry, hostile self that is redeemed. Our failure to receive this good news where it really applies is due to our failure to come clean—to expose the unacceptable self. Or perhaps our inability to come clean—to expose the unacceptable self—is due to our failure to appropriate the good news. The mutuality between the gospel and confession makes it difficult to determine in instances of blockage which is the chicken and which is the egg. It takes the good news of God's unconditional love to give one the courage to confront his own unacceptableness, and it takes a willingness to face the unacceptable in himself before one can realize the good news of God's unconditional love.

The unacceptable may not always be anger. It may be an unsanctioned sexual attraction, an ulterior motive, a clandestine indulgence in erotic fantasy, or even an acting out of hidden desires in a double life. When the pastor is counseling with a person who is suffering from mental anguish, whose conscience is supersensitive to his apparent shortcomings, and who receives no comfort for the gospel, he should be alert to the possibility that his counselee is of a double mind. Despite the obvious sincerity and openness of the sufferer, there is probably a hidden and opposing mind for which the only manifestation is this seemingly irrational blockage to reconciliation.

When the conscience is "under the law" one cannot deal straightforwardly with hate. For this he needs the atmosphere of grace. Nor can he acknowledge his own duplicity. Suffering is the price he pays to keep his two minds apart and intact. The gospel of grace demands not only a confrontation between these two minds but also a decision regarding them that would unify the person. The gospel redeems us from the bondage to the law— a bondage in which the conformist and the rebellious minds maintain somewhat independent identities within the same person. The goal is freedom through love. God's purpose in his redemption is not to set aside the law but rather to enable us to fulfill the law from "the heart." The gospel unites through love the person divided by judgment.

When one's self is divided by the judgment of the law, he is hindered in establishing relationships. Honest anger is not a problem in relationships as much as the avoidance of anger and the subsequent scapegoating of substitutes. For those most hindered in their expression, the scapegoat is often themselves. The depressions they experience are forms of self-berating which compensate for their unexpressed anger toward others.

When we have hidden our anger, we tend to avoid intimacy with others because such closeness would threaten to expose what is hidden. The crisis that might ensue could seem intolerable. For this reason people with hidden hostilities may approach sexual intimacy in marriage with ambivalence. Sex as a substitute for a relationship is something different than sex as an expression of a relationship. By the same taken, people with hidden hostilities toward God may have ambivalence over the Sacrament of Holy Communion regardless of how religious they may consider themselves to be. Intimacy is a problem for them because it provokes both desire and repulsion.

I know a bereaved father who admitted his indignation against "the sorry scheme of things entire" in the tragic death of his son. He was probably closer to God than one who in a similar condition would feel compelled to stifle his indignation by saying, "The Lord gave, and the Lord has taken away; blest be the name of the Lord." This father went on to say that it helped him in his grief to be angry. I believe Job would agree. The opposite of love is not anger or even hate, but indifference and not caring. Anger is an expression of vitality, even if negative, and as such is a form of caring.

While there is an acceptance of anger in the Christian tradition, there is also a judgment upon it. "Everyone who is angry with his brother," says Jesus, "shall be liable to the judgment." Some ancient manuscripts insert the phrase, "without cause." While the original interpretation of this phrase is open to question, a modern interpretation would be the displacement phenomenon. When our anger is displaced to convenient objects because we feel unable to express it in the original context, we are scapegoating and under the judgment of being angry with our brother without cause.

Anger like other passions needs to be disciplined. Too often, however, discipline is associated with denial rather than direction. "Be angry," says the apostle Paul, "but do not sin." Angry feelings like sexual feelings are not sinful in themselves. It is what we do with them that is under judgment. Basic to any wholesome discipline of these feelings is our acceptance of anger as such and our awareness of what stimulates it in any given situation.

3. ACCEPTANCE OF ANGER AND DESPAIR

It is easier for a counselor to deal with guilt and anxiety in his counselee than despair and resentment. Since Job expressed the latter, his counselors were discomfited and in self-defense pressured him to express, instead, the former. Guilt and anxiety appear to the counselor to be simpler to handle. We are inclined by our own defense system to use reassurance as our therapeutic resource. Guilt and anxiety, because they are "hurting" experiences, naturally call for reassurance. "God will forgive—everything is going to be all right—we all love you." On the other hand, hostility and despair are attacking experiences and naturally repel the hearer. Despair of course is also a "hurting" experience, but its hopelessness is a defiance against any therapeutic resource.

Whenever guilt and anxiety are cover-ups for hostility and despair, their simplicity is a ruse. Reassurance, therefore, does not reassure because it is directed only to the surface expression. What is needed is a deeper searching into the nature of the guilt and anxiety in spite of the apparent pain this causes. It was precisely this kind of pain that the three friends could not endure. They lacked the courage to respond. If we can judge them on the basis of our own reluctance to respond, they were afraid to go down with Job into the depths of his pain because the rope might break. What would begin as a response to Job's feelings might stir up their own. The latent fear is that we will see ourselves in the sufferer, and the doubts we have kept in containment may break out and overwhelm us.

The counselor needs to identify with the counselee. Otherwise there is no common ground of sharing. Yet he also needs to be somewhat objective. Otherwise there will be two who need help instead of one. The idea is to put one foot down to the emotional depths of the counselee while keeping the other foot on solid ground. Our fear is that in putting the one foot down we shall lose our balance and fall into the problem pit ourselves. When we overidentify with our counselee, it is probably because the relationship has aroused some sleeping dogs within us.

While underidentification is a defense against overidentification, it is hardly the solution. In our under-identification, we are like the three friends in that we attempt to "set people straight" without empathy or even as a substitute for empathy. The problem which we do not share seems more simple than it actually is; hence the ease with which we produce the answer and the difficulty with which the counselee accepts it. The following description of a pastor's hospital visit is an example of this reluctance to empathize when feelings are expressed that seem threatening at the moment.

Pastor: Good evening. I am Pastor Doe. May I be of service to you in any way?

Patient: Yes, I would like to visit with you. I've felt very lonely today.

Pastor: What seems to be the problem? (He is aware of a need but bypasses the feelings of loneliness.)

Patient: My family hasn't been in yet today. I sure miss my kids! They aren't permitted to come in the room, but my wife comes every day and it really helps a lot. I've been here for two weeks now and I would like to go home and rest.

Pastor: You feel you have been recovering quite well since your operation? (He bypasses the feelings of homesickness to twist out a positive implication.)

Patient: Oh, I'm still pretty weak, but I guess that is to be expected following a major operation.

Pastor: It takes time to recover after major surgery. (This response would be acceptable in itself except that in the pattern that the pastor is establishing, it constitutes another attempt to avoid dealing with the patient's feelings.)

Patient: I can't figure out why I haven't been permitted to walk around yet. . . . It seems like the longer I stay in bed the weaker I get.

Pastor: You feel the hospital could allow you a little more freedom in getting up and around? (He avoids the patient's apprehensions about the progress of his recovery and focuses instead on hospital procedure.)

Patient: The only thing is that it costs so much to remain in a hospital nowadays; in fact, a person can hardly afford to get sick anymore—especially when you don't have very good insurance.

Pastor: You feel the worry over money is affecting your recovery? (Worry over money is more tangible and less threatening; so he deals with it.)

Patient: Yes, that's the reason I'd like to get out of here as soon as possible. But I guess I'm caught in one of those things you just don't have any control over. I can't help but wonder why it happened to me.

Pastor: It makes you think when it hits so close to home. (He avoids the patient's disturbing question concerning God's ways and offers instead a related but overused cliché.)

Patient: I guess a person never realizes how lucky he is when all is going well. I guess we take it all for granted and forget how thankful we should be for health and all the good things in life.

Pastor: Many of us do not appreciate how fortunate we are until something goes wrong for us! (He feels more comfortable with this expression of a common guilt and seconds the motion.)

(pause.)

Patient: Yes, a person has a lot of time to think about life in a place like this; guess it is pretty easy to get so busy that you never think much except about the everyday problems we have. (pause.) I guess there might be something good about getting sick as well as something bad.

Pastor: You feel you can learn from such an experience as you're having? (He is quick to pick up this opportunity to interpret the illness positively.)

Patient: Maybe so, but how can God do this to me? (The patient objects to this pressure for a simple solution.)

Pastor: You think God wanted you to suffer like this? (When hit head-on, he accepts the negative interpretation but in a resistance way.)

Patient: What else can I think? (Patient feels defensive after the pastor's previous response.)

Pastor: God loves all of us, even when we are upset with him. (Enough of this! The pastor has the answer!)

Patient: Does God love me now? (Patient tries again to express his existential problem over the pastor's "solution.")

Pastor: Yes. (no debate.)

Patient: How do you know? (Patient resists this simple affirmation from one who does not have the problem—asks "by what authority?")

Pastor: The Bible and Jesus tell us of this truth. (He quotes the authorities.)

Patient: That helps. (At least he has the weight of respected tradition behind him—and the patient ceases his resistance.)

Pastor: I've enjoyed talking with you today. I'll try and stop by
          and see you again before you leave the hospital. (Grateful
          for this bit of acquiescence on the part of the patient, he
          takes this opportunity for an exit.)

Patient: I would appreciate that very much.

Pastor: Good night.

The patient was worried about his recovery and was asking
why this sickness had happened to him. We miss the compassion that should be evident on the part of the pastor to the
despair of the patient. The pastor is more like Job's three
friends. Much of what he said—like much of what they said—
was true. The point is that his truth was given in the presence of
a mood that made it unfitting. He made little identification with
this mood. Therefore, it is doubtful if the patient could identify
with the pastor's help.

The frightening aspect of anger and the hopeless aspect of
despair are repellents to any conversation. To respond to them
requires courage. It demands involvement in the unpleasant
questions for which we may have no answers. The pastor may
agree intellectually that it is helpful for people to share these
feelings, and yet find himself emotionally unprepared to permit
it. We are reluctant to enter into any involvement over which we
have no control, and so prefer to exercise our controls beforehand
to prevent things from going too far. This is particularly true
when despair and hostility are held in check within our own
bosom. We see the giants in the promised land and lose our
courage—preferring instead the safety of the repugnant wilder-
ness.

Yet acceptance of people means also an acceptance of their
hostility and despair. This acceptance helps the counselee to
look further into his frightened and unacceptable self. When

such acceptance is given, the result is none of the things which the pastor had feared. As is so often the case, the giants were built up by his own apprehensions. Acceptance does not open the door to the severing of relationship ties, nor does it lower the mental image that each has of the other. Actually it is the pastor's emotional resistance to such sharing that weakens the ties and lowers the mental images. Job's experience with his three friends is a case in point. After the seven days of empathetic silence, Job anticipated his counselors' acceptance. When they refused to accept his expression of despair, he was disappointed in them. His mental image of them was negatively altered and the relationship ties were strained.

When the counselee drops hints of inner disturbance, he looks for the green light from the pastor to proceed. He is asking for some assurance of acceptance before he can risk further exposure. When the patient in the preceding dialogue said, "I wonder why this is happening to me," he was in effect saying, "You are a pastor and I am having a religious problem. I am concerned about whether or not I will recover, and as I lie here I keep wondering why God is doing this to me—why am I being singled out?"

The pastor who takes his cue from the Book of Job will open himself to the patient at this point. Not that it will be easy, for the question is one he would rather not hear. Most pastors feel their position as pastors threatened when someone questions God's ways. This is why responding to such feelings requires courage. Yet if the patient's needs come first, the pastor must respond. When he understands that it is by sharing rather than by repressing these disturbing feelings that healing takes place, his love for the sufferer may provide the courage.

The presence of inner disturbance is not always so directly expressed as by this hospital patient. Nor does the counselee himself always realize what it is that is disturbing him. The source of disturbing feelings is more easily repressed than the feelings themselves. The person may only know that he feels uncomfortable. If he can be encouraged to share this fact with the counselor, the topic of conversation at the moment is a clue to the source of the tension. "I'm not sure why," he might say, "but right now I feel tense. In fact I want to get up and leave." The counselor might respond, "It probably has something to do with what we are talking about. Shall we stay with it? It may be significant."

The counselee who is willing to inform the counselor of his hidden discomfort will usually be willing to take on the challenge. In exposing his hidden feelings, he is breaking with whatever ambivalence he had about coming to grips with his problem. He is demonstrating his sincerity. The procedure is reminiscent of the children's game in which the searcher for the hidden object is given hints by the one who has hidden it who says *cold, warm,* or *hot* depending upon how close the searcher is. The difference, of course, is that the counselee may not know what it is that is hidden but only the telltale discomfort—*hot.*

Sometimes the counselee's nonverbal communication of disturbance is so obvious that the pastor can respond to it rather than to the verbal communication. He may say, "You are irritated," or "you wonder whether there is any use"—depending upon what is being communicated through the countenance. In this way he flips out into the open that which was directly beneath the surface. The counselee is often relieved for this assist and grateful for the understanding. The greater openness reduces the sense of mystery and enhances the potential for overcoming.

Job's hostility as well as his despair were out in the open. The three friends were discomfited by this and did their best to stifle him but were not successful. Job stuck his neck out. He risked their wrath and their threats. By giving expression to the way he felt he exposed himself to judgment. Concerned primarily with justice rather than safety, he let go rather than hold back. As he himself said, "I will speak, and let come what may. I will take my flesh in my teeth and put my life in my hand." In so doing he was an example of that daring use of the tongue that Kierkegaard said divided the men from the boys. The safe thing to do is to keep quiet, for people will rarely judge you for what you do *not* say. He who dares to speak exposes himself to judgment. "To be silent," says Kierkegaard, "is the easy way." Yet for this reason it is "the most dangerous thing of all." [2] One remains safe, and hence unjudged, at the expense of his growth in selfhood.

Because Job defies their intimidations, the three friends were coerced into prolonged arguments. But at least they stayed with the subject. They judged Job and they evaded the critical issue of his complaint, but they remained in the general area of his problem. They could have done worse by changing the subject, remaining silent, giving evasive reassurance, or taking their leave. Instead they expressed their irritation and argued passionately. At least they *cared*. Because Job had the temerity to fight back, he got his feelings out, even if defiantly.

The three friends tried with all the weight of tradition and intimidation to coerce guilt from Job. Instead they got more hostility. If they had been acceptive of Job's hostility and empathetic toward his despair, they might have prepared the way for him to take a more realistic look at himself. Instead they pressed for a confession and Job resisted their coercion. Their approach changed the issue for Job from one of sharing to one of preserving his integrity. His refusal to bow to force made it difficult for him to admit any inadequacy in himself. Such an admission would have been a sign of weakness, of compromise,

[2] *Sickness unto Death*, p. 167.

to obtain mercy. For a person of Job's ego strength, this would have been tantamount to selling his soul to save his life. It would have meant the loss of the one thing that neither his calamities nor his tormentors could take from him, namely, his self-respect. As Viktor Frankl has observed, the last freedom that one has is the freedom to choose his attitude toward his own sufferings. This is the last expression of human dignity and therefore the actual essence of human dignity. It is to Job's credit that he refused to surrender it.

If the three friends could not accept his immediate sense of outrage, he would not confide to them his more ambiguous feelings concerning his shortcomings. Acceptance takes one further into the unacceptable. For Job the most threatening feelings were not those of anger but of guilt. It remained for the fourth counselor, Elihu, to take him to this deeper level. If the three friends are helpful to us in illustrating how not to minister, Elihu is helpful in demonstrating a more effective way.

There has been a recent reaction against counseling as *responding*. The critics say that responding is not enough; there is also *confronting*. The counselee needs direction and not simply a sounding board for his feelings. These objections are valid. They become invalid, however, when their proponents fail to appreciate the value in responding. Counseling as responding is inadequate in itself. There is also the need for confrontation and direction. Yet counseling as responding is essential to counseling as confronting.

The danger in all reactions is that, in correcting an abuse, one fails to recognize any worth in the system he is correcting. Consequently he falls into error in the opposite extreme. One can place an overemphasis on confrontation also. The counselor who confronts must also respond. The pastor who leads must also be the pastor who follows. Otherwise he may find himself so far in the lead that no one is following.

At the same time the pastor who follows must also be prepared to lead. Otherwise he may fail to offer the counselee the stimulus of challenge at the opportune moment. Confrontation also requires courage. The Book of Job has something to say about this courage also. It offers the balance in pastoral care that is needed to hold both emphases in creative tension.

IX

ELIHU—THE DIFFERENCE

Job 32–37

When the words of Job were ended and the three friends ceased to answer Job because he was righteous in his own eyes, Job was driven up the wall in defensiveness. Like a cat with its hair on end, he was in no way open to receive from God or man. The Elihu discourses are the transition from Job bristling with defiance to Job open to the revelation out of the whirlwind. While some textual critics believe the Elihu discourses to be an interpolation by a later author, from a pastoral theological viewpoint they are needed to account for the movement of the drama. The fact that there is no mention of Elihu in the epilogue is difficult to explain if there were a single author to the book. On the other hand, it is even more difficult from a pastoral point of view to account for the openness of Job to divine revelation without the transition of the Elihu speeches.

1. THE TRANSITION FROM THE DIALOGUES TO GOD

The approach of Elihu at the termination of the dialogues was the needed influence to take Job off the defensive. While there is much in Elihu that sounds like the three friends, there are also specifically pastoral differences that can account for the contrast between resistance and openness in Job. The three friends had God in a box. Their dogmatic attitude allowed for no unsolved problems nor unanswered questions. After Job's belabored whitewash of his character, they gave up on him. "What's the use—the man's hopeless!" They had been given the power to love, but instead they had judged.

In contrast to the cut and dried approach of the three friends, Elihu allowed for mystery in the universe. He is impartial in a negative sort of way, being angry at both Job and the three friends. "He was angry at Job because he justified himself rather than God; he was angry also at Job's three friends because they had found no answer, although they had declared Job to be in the wrong." In spite of his negative impartiality, Elihu is positive in his concern about Job's problem and in his conviction that he has something to contribute to its solution.

Elihu had to wait until the other three were finished because they were older than he, and he believed that he should let "many years teach wisdom." Many words came but little wisdom. Elihu was disillusioned with longevity. "It is not the old that are wise," he concluded, "nor the aged that understand what is right." We are reminded of Kierkegaard's observation that whatever it may be that one comes to as a matter of course because of his years, it is not wisdom. In fact, it is precisely wisdom that he may lose with the years. Whatever fear or respect had kept Elihu quiet was now overcome by his indignation at the folly of these elders. He wanted in! "Therefore I say, 'Listen to me; let me also declare my opinion.'"

2. STRUCTURING THE RELATIONSHIP

Once he had the floor Elihu immediately dissociated himself from the three friends. One would assume that he were allied with them had he not clarified his position. In pastoral counseling this is called *structuring*. If he were to get through to Job he had to demonstrate his impartiality. Otherwise Job would automatically project onto him the mental image he had of the three friends, and the resistance would have been impenetrable. The situation is similar to that in which a pastor finds himself when a family asks him to talk to its erring member. "I'm sure, Pastor, if you talk to my husband—or son—he'll listen." The pastor is not nearly so sure. He knows the deck is already stacked against him. He approaches such a person as an ally of those who are "on his back" until he proves otherwise. A verbal structuring of his position is the first step in this direction. It secures the attention that is necessary before anything can be proved.

Thus Elihu made his position clear. He had waited, he said, for the three friends to give Job an answer, but they had failed. He even warned them against assuming that they had God on their side. Since Job had not directed his words against *him,* Elihu will not answer him with their speeches.

Elihu's charge that none of the three had spoken directly to Job's need is substantially correct. Furthermore they were now discomfited and silenced. Why should he wait any longer when they stand there with not a word to say? Besides, he himself has so much to say! He is "full of words" and passion. His spirit constrains him to speak, for his "heart is like wine that has no vent; like new wineskins, it is ready to burst." Therefore he must speak to relieve his own pressure.

At least Elihu is honest enough to admit his own involvement. He is anything but disinterested, and he is speaking for his own sake as well as Job's. The man obviously cares. He is concerned about what has been going on and wants to get involved.

Yet once more he affirms his impartiality—probably because

Job had made such a protest against the partiality of the three friends. Elihu will flatter no one! Why? Because if he did, his Maker would put an end to him! His motive for being honest is his fear of God. Job would understand this. He gave the same motive as proof for his own innocence. From the way he looked at a virgin to the way he treated his servants, he was governed by his sense of accountability to God. "What shall I do when God rises up?" Also Job had accused the three friends of forsaking the fear of God because of their bias and careless use of words against him.

In pastoral counseling Elihu's appeal to the same motivation as Job is an example of *identifying* with the counselee. Such identification is the basis upon which rapport is established and the relationship initiated. By thus identifying with Job, Elihu could communicate his sincerity. "But now, hear my speech, O Job, . . . my words declare the uprightness of my heart, and what my lips know they speak sincerely."

3. HIS ATMOSPHERE OF ACCEPTANCE

Within this atmosphere of genuine concern Elihu invited Job to speak his mind. "Answer me, if you can; . . . take your stand." There is no need to hesitate, for "I am toward God as you are; I too was formed from a piece of clay." By putting himself on the same plane with Job, Elihu was disavowing any attempt to coerce. Job had nothing to fear from him because they were two of a kind. Elihu's apparent lack of humility in his confidence in his own opinions is balanced by the candid admission of his own human finitude. He does not intend to attack Job. "Behold, no fear of me need terrify you; my pressure will not be heavy upon you." Such assurance of acceptance must have been quite impressive to Job after what he had been through with the other three.

The fact that Elihu states he was present during the dialogues gives weight to his offer of acceptance. Sometimes we offer such acceptance without really knowing what it is we are accepting. Since the recipient knows we do not know, he cannot really trust our offer. Job knows that Elihu has witnessed his worst. If he can offer to accept him after all this, he must really care about him.

This is not to say that Elihu had no criticism of Job's behavior. Acceptance does not preclude value judgments. In fact the compulsion to avoid value judgments can be as unacceptive as the compulsion to give them. If we accept a person we are concerned about what he *does*. His behavior is not a matter beyond our interest. The good news of God's acceptance, for example, is that God loves us in spite of his disapproval of some of our ways. The old idea that we hate the sin but love the sinner is still valid. If the one we love is harming himself by what he does, we are constrained by compassion to confront him about his behavior.

After structuring his approach as one of impartiality and acceptance, Elihu proceeded to restate Job's argument. Since Job had spoken in his hearing, he was in a position to do this. "You say, 'I am clean, without transgression; I am pure, and there is no iniquity in me.'" The fault as Job saw it was in God: You say, "'he finds occasions against me, he counts me as his enemy.'" This is a fair restatement of Job's position.

In pastoral counseling the use of restatement is a technique for facilitating communication. If the pastor restates or reflects in his own words what the counselee has communicated, he is demonstrating that he understands. This in turn gives the green light to the counselee to share more. Also in case the pastor was mistaken in his understanding, the counselee has the opportunity to set him straight.

Elihu's restatement of Job's position at the beginning of their relationship got things off on a common basis. Job had the evidence that he had gotten through. Even though Elihu—or any counselor—may disagree with his counselee's position, the fact that he can restate that position before he disagrees shows he has established contact in a rational rather than an emotional manner. We can take disagreement much better if we are first assured that we have been understood.

Having restated Job's position Elihu proceeded to confront him with his disagreement. "Behold, in this you are not right." Here was a simple, straightforward, honest confrontation Furthermore he will tell Job why he believes as he does. "I will answer you." Elihu is concerned that Job has a defensive and limited point of view that could cause him to miss out on God's communication. "For God speaks in one way, and in two, though man does not perceive it." Job needs to consider this. In dreams, visions of the night, and other ways God attempts to open one's ears. And why? That he may keep "back his soul from the Pit." God's purposes in all his ways with man are redemptive.

Elihu not only expressed his disagreement with Job, but also presented an alternative. His procedure is an effective demonstration of the technique of confrontation in pastoral counseling. Furthermore the alternative which he presented is his emphasis throughout. Job, he believes, may be missing the big issue in his trial, namely, what is God saying through it? Rather than concluding, "God will answer none of my words," Job might consider whether God *is* answering but not in ways that Job is predisposed to recognize.

4. IDENTIFIES JOB WITH HUMANITY'S PREDICAMENT

What follows is a clear example of how Elihu differs from the three friends. They had tried to put the label of sinner upon Job. Only in this way could they account for his calamities. Elihu, on the other hand, identifies Job with humanity. It is *man* who is chastened with pain upon his bed—not outstanding sinners. Suffering is a human predicament with a redemptive potential. It is man whose life loathes bread so that his flesh is wasted away—whose bones stick out and whose soul draws near to the Pit. The description is obviously that of Job, but the subject is humanity. By this identification Elihu removed the stigma from Job that the three friends placed upon him. He took away the accusing finger that made him a special and evil case. The humanity that encompassed Job also included Elihu.

In striking contrast to the three friends, Elihu identified himself with Job's predicament. By the same token he identified himself also with his hope. The common human experience of "drawing near the Pit" stimulates a longing for the Messiah-mediator. As Elihu expressed it, "If there be for him a mediator!" In language akin to New Testament images of redemption he expressed the hope for a gracious word that would say, "Deliver him from going down into the Pit, I have found a ransom."

Elihu is again manifesting himself in contrast to the three friends who had no need for a Christ figure. They had the answers. It was Job who lacked the answers and hence hoped for a mediator. Elihu joined him. The humble have room for Christ. They do not know it all. Their lowliness is shown in their acceptance of mystery; they are open for revelation and redemption.

Elihu pictures this redemption in terms of bodily health. Let the flesh that was wasted away become fresh with youth. The healing of the soul carries over to the body. There is no dynamic for healing more potent than gratitude. When man prays to God and God accepts him, he enters into God's presence with joy. He shares with his fellowman the good news of his salvation. His praising of God is an expression of his health. A familiar passage in Isaiah has a similar emphasis: "They who wait for the Lord shall renew their strength, they shall mount up with wings like eagles, they shall run and not be weary, they shall walk and not faint." The Old Testament emphasizes the unity of man in each of his parts. The body is also a beneficiary of the soul's redemption from the Pit.

As Elihu pictures the anticipated redemption, God's forgiveness precedes the sinner's repentance. It is after he experiences divine deliverance that the sufferer says, "I sinned, and perverted what was right, and it was not requited to me." In terms of the categories of law and gospel, it is not only the law that prepares the way for the gospel, but the gospel also prepares the way for the law. Repentance, in contrast to despair, is sorrow with *hope*. Hope is generated by experience. The hope for forgiveness is inseparable from forgiveness itself. "He has redeemed my soul from going down into the Pit, and my life shall see the light."

Elihu's portrayal of redemption is not something that happens once, but rather is a repeated experience in the life of the redeemed. "Behold, God does all these things, twice, three times, with a man, to bring back his soul from the Pit, that he may see the light of life." Being plunged to the edge of the Pit and being divinely delivered to a renewal of hope corresponds to the New Testament concepts of crucifixion and resurrection. We grow in our redemption by becoming identified with Christ in the crucifixion of the old man, so that we may become identified with him also in the resurrection to the new man whose life is in the Spirit. This identification with Christ in his crucifixion and resurrection is a recurrent and an existential experience in our sanctification.

Having given expression to his own views concerning Job's predicament, Elihu again invites Job to join in dialogue with him. "If you have anything to say, answer me." To show he meant what he said, he gave him a reason. "Speak, for I desire to justify you." Elihu tries to communicate his good faith. I'm not out simply to nail you to the wall, Job. I'm on your side. I want to work this thing out together with you.

In spite of the encouraging invitation Job gave no reply. Why is he silent now when he was so vocal before? Obviously the literary style of the book is altered in the Elihu discourses. Yet the dynamics of the drama may have something to do with this. Pastorally speaking, Job may be talked out. Elihu's approach must have been refreshing to him after the defensive reactions of the three friends. Having had his say, he may now be more interested in having Elihu carry on.

Elihu is not hesitant to do so. If you are not going to come in, Job, then listen to me. "Be silent, and I will teach you wisdom." In expressing such complete confidence in the worth of his remarks he displays anything but modesty. Yet our association of modesty with self-effacement makes it difficult for us to recognize conceit. Elihu obviously believes he has something to say. To admit it openly may exhibit more humility than to be apologetic about it. The point at issue is how much we associate humility with honesty. In believing he had something to offer, Elihu may be voicing the confidence of a pastor. He is a man with a message!

Job's reticence seems to have given Elihu a sense of conquest. Invited by the silence to carry on, he began to manifest the corruption of power. First, however, he restates Job's position again. "For Job has said, 'I am innocent, and God has taken away my right . . . my wound is incurable, though I am without transgression.'" Although the restatement is again fairly objective, what follows is reminiscent of the three friends. "What man is like Job, who drinks up scoffing like water?"

5. ELIHU'S CONCERN IN HIS CRITICISM

Job's charge that "it profits a man nothing that he should take delight in God," irritated Elihu. He took to God's defense with all the force of Eliphaz. "Far be it from God that he should do wickedness, and from the Almighty that he should do wrong." Is there any difference between this kind of criticism and that of the three friends? So far as the actual words spoken, obviously not. If we look into the purpose for saying them, however, the answer may be different.

Elihu's purpose is not so much to pin the label of sinner on Job as to defend God against Job's accusations. His defense of God, however questionable, is more for God's sake than for his own. In contrast to the three friends who were threatened by the charge, Elihu is appalled at Job's lack of confidence in God. Consequently, even in his attack he focuses more upon the central issues in Job's predicament than did the three friends. His defense of God is less egocentric and more theocentric than that of Eliphaz, but it is less Job-centered than his previous approach. His difference, therefore, is in attitude and timing rather than in wording. In pastoral counseling this is an important difference. Attitude and timing have precedence over wording even as the spirit of the counselor has precedence over his techniques.

Elihu's primary concern in his attack on Job is with defending God against Job's charge of partiality. God, he insists, shows no partiality to princes and regards the poor the same as the rich. In fact it is God who is keeping us all going. "If he would gather to himself his breath, all flesh would perish together." Actually it is Job who is asking God to be partial. In demanding that God appoint a time for him to have a hearing, he was asking for special privilege. God is not accountable to man. He is not simply an anthropomorphic projection of a king who sits in the gate at the appointed time to hear the people's grievances. When God is quiet, who—man or nation—can fault him? When he hides his face, who can behold him? Despite the mystery of his ways, Elihu believes that God's purpose throughout is the defense of the poor against their oppressors—"that a godless man should not reign."

In contrast to Job's demand of God that he be given a hearing, Elihu asks, "Has any one said to God, 'I have borne chastisement; I will not offend any more; teach me what I do not see; if I have done iniquity, I will do it no more'?" This is what he would like to see happen with Job. Yet he will not coerce because the decision is Job's. "For you must choose, and not I." Knowing where the responsibility lies, he respects Job's freedom as a person.

When Elihu entered into the dialogue it was stated that he was angry not only with the three friends for not answering Job but also with Job for justifying himself rather than God. Some of this anger is undoubtedly coming out in this second discourse. When one is bent on self-justification, he becomes offensive to others.

Anger must have been Elihu's feeling when he concluded that men of understanding would say to him that Job's words were without insight, and that because he added rebellion to his sins, he should be tried to the end. Although he attributes this sentiment to others, he is probably giving vent to his own feelings.

When we hear someone speak in an arrogant way, we almost wish he would get his deserved penalty. Few of us create much sympathy by the way in which we quarrel. During a tense moment in the negotiations at the conclusion of the Korean War, a North Korean diplomat pointed his gun at an American military negotiator. The American was shocked. "Where's your dignity?" he demanded! Diplomats may quarrel with dignity, but who else?

6. ELIHU TALKS TO THE ISSUE

After a second invitation to Job to "declare what he knows," Elihu began what could be considered his third discourse. When Job was again silent, he carried through on his promise not only to criticize but also to answer Job. He began by again re-stating Job's position. "You ask, 'What advantage have I? How am I better off than if I had sinned?'" Now we are at the heart of the matter. "Does Job fear God for nought?" The three friends had evaded the question. Elihu with characteristic courage "zeroes in" on it: "I will answer you."

How is Job in all his calamities any better off for having covenanted himself to God than he would have been were he uncommitted? To Job's three friends his calamities simply indi-cated he had broken the covenant. In contrast Elihu accepts Job's question as valid. The problem, he says, is in Job's tendency to anthropomorphize God. He thought of God as the Big One among many little ones. In the language of Paul Tillich, God for Job was a Being in the midst of beings, rather than Being itself. His image of God had become contaminated with projec-tions based upon human interactions. "Your wickedness and your righteousness," says Elihu, "concern people like yourself. They add nothing to God." Because things have gone wrong for Job he was assuming that God was dealing with him as the King of the land. He had it "in" for him and was retaliating by torment-ing him.

After extricating God from Job's anthropomorphic projections, Elihu continued his attempt to answer Job by analyzing the human reaction to suffering. "Because of the multitude of op-pressions people cry out; they call for help because of the arm of the mighty." This is a description of "foxhole religion." When the masses are in the midst of stress, they cry for help to the One who is bigger than they. There are no atheists in the fox-holes. In contrast, "none says, 'Where is God my Maker, who gives songs in the night?'" *"Songs* in the *night"* indicates joy in the midst of trouble. "We ask not for lighter burdens," says a familiar prayer, "but for stronger backs." The truly religious person is not the one who cries for help in trouble. This is the natural human reaction to stress. Rather, the truly religious person believes that God can sustain in the midst of stress.

Obviously it is this deeper level of religious insight that Elihu wants to see in Job, even though only a few achieve it. The cry of the multitude is an empty cry. It shows no depth in faith, and the Almighty does not regard it. You have joined the multitudes, Job, when you say you do not see God—when you say "that the case is before him, and you are waiting for him!" Are you not closing your eyes to where God may be and your ears to what he may be speaking? Besides, it is rather audacious for the creature to "pan" his Creator. The fact that you are able to say these things, Job, is an example of the very acceptance of God that you are denying.

Job undoubtedly realized God's acceptance but did so defiantly. Perhaps he was testing it. His feelings toward God were am-bivalent; he desired him and yet was angry toward him. In his defensive frame of mind he was not about to admit any awareness of God's acceptance because he did not care to give any quarter in the contest. God to Job is also the Antagonist. His attraction for God is matched by his resistance to him.

To Elihu Job is experiencing a *human* predicament. Rather than being singled out for arbitrary punishment, he is being challenged to a wider vision. It is not that God withdraws his eyes from the righteous as Job has charged; rather, he treats them as kings upon the throne. But even "kings are bound in fetters and caught in the cords of affliction." It can happen to any of us—including Elihu. If it does, God is present in a positive way. He is opening the ears to instruction so that one may hear what before he did not hear and consequently become more aware of his shortcomings and of his challenge to grow. "He delivers the afflicted by their affliction, and opens their ear by adversity."

Since suffering can come upon the righteous, it is not a punishment for sinners. Running throughout Elihu's argument is the theme, "No one is good but God alone" (Luke 18:19). His approach to suffering is at the heart of the pastoral care of the sick. The pastor is not only a consoler to the sick but also a mediator. His goal is not only healing but also redemption. In differentiation from other members of the healing team, his concern is to assist the sick in hearing what God is saying through their illness. He offers himself as a person with whom the patient can share his feelings and search for meaning. The relationship that is established is a dynamic through which the Holy Spirit operates. As such it is a cogent example of how Christ the intangible head communicates through the sharing of the tangible members in his Body, the Church.

Elihu cautions Job against reacting in opposite extremes to his frustrations. He had noted Job's initial tendency to give up and long for death. "Do not long for the night, when peoples are cut off in their place." When Job would emerge from this despair of weakness, he went to the opposite extreme and despaired in defiance. Yet attacking God is not the answer either. "Take heed, do not turn to iniquity, for this you have chosen rather than affliction." Having gotten both extremes of immature behavior out of his system, perhaps Job is ready now to accept his situation in the strength of a new vision.

With this, Elihu turned his attention from Job to God, and, inviting Job to join him, began to marvel at the Creator's ways. God's handiwork in nature was the most tangible image of God to which Elihu could point. Here was the mask through which a receptive Job could perceive his God. His words anticipate Job's encounter with God. It is the beginning of Elihu's fade-away, as he becomes lost in his own gaze into God's glory. He is like John the Baptist who prepared the way for the Lord and then decreased with the increase of the Lord. He is a pastor whose purpose is to lead his people to their encounter with God and then to step aside.

"Can any one understand the spreading of the clouds, the thunderings of his pavilion?" Why does God do all these marvelous and fearful things? Elihu presents three purposes for God's mighty acts. "Whether for correction, or for his land, or for love, he causes it to happen." That God's purpose is love points forward to the ultimate significance of the coming theophany. Yet before this there is correction. Is Job so sure he wants his day in court? "Shall it be told him that I would speak?" Elihu warns Job that he was asking for more than he antici-pated. "Did a man ever wish that he would be swallowed up?"

Elihu's prediction concerning Job's reaction to God's revelation has a New Testament parallel in the reaction of the apostle Thomas to the Lord's resurrection. Thomas had told the other disciples that he could not believe that the Lord was risen unless he could see in his hands the print of the nails and place his finger in the mark of the nails. When the Lord later stood before Thomas and invited him to touch, the apostle was overwhelmed with the reality of the Lord's presence. He had neither desire nor need to touch. Instead he said, "My Lord and my God." So also with Job. When he got his chance all he could say was, "I lay my hand upon my mouth." He had not realized for what he was asking.

7. DIFFERENCE IN ATTITUDE AND PERSPECTIVE

The difference between Elihu and the three friends is in attitude and perspective. Though his content and technique at times parallel those of the others, Elihus' concern throughout is that Job take a wider look at his problem lest he miss out on what God has to say. It is the setting that constitutes the difference. Elihu himself knew this and made it clear from the beginning. "He had not directed his words against me, and I will not answer him with your speeches. . . . The spirit within me constrains me . . . and what my lips know they speak sincerely." There were times when he deviated from these objectives and answered Job "with their speeches." But words themselves are not the only factors in communication. They may even be subsidiary to attitudes and intentions. Elihu's perspective is obviously different from that of the others, and it is within this perspective that his words are communicated.

We have in this differentiation a possible clue to a difficult problem in pastoral care. What is the difference between pastoral counseling and secular counseling—between what a pastor says in a counseling session and what a clinical psychologist or psychiatric case worker says? If we base the difference on words or techniques, we would be forced to say that a pastor uses words such as God, and "religious" procedures such as prayer and Bible reading. Yet he may have a genuine pastoral conversation without using "religious" words or techniques, or he may even use these as a substitute for pastoral conversation.

Obviously pastors and other counselors may use similar techniques and words. The difference is in the perspective of the counselor. The nature of the profession itself projects a distinctive perspective in terms of goals. Yet even within the same profession the counselor's perspectives may vary. Elihu, for example, was no more professionally a pastor than the other three. Yet his hope for a mediator predisposed him to a different perspective than that of the three friends who used "religious terminology," but were humanists in their possession of God.

When the perspectives of the counselors differ, we can expect different results, though their techniques may at times parallel one another. The question not only concerns counseling techniques, but the service to which the techniques are used. Here is the issue that makes for the qualitative difference. Like so many matters of the spirit, the difference is not always identifiable by tangible earmarks. It is the total process that tells the story rather than any particular cross section. The counseling dynamic involves the intangible as well as the tangible. In terms of communication the intangible influence of attitudes and perspectives is crucial. It is a highly directive influence regardless of how non-directive or directive may be the techniques employed.

X

THE COURAGE TO CONFRONT

Whenever a group of pastors are assembled to hear about the methodology of pastoral counseling, sooner or later one of them is bound to ask, "But aren't there times when we just *tell* the person?" The tone of his voice indicates that he is chafing at the limitations of responsive listening. Like Elihu he is "full of words" and "he must speak, that he may find relief."

Telling is the most used method of communication. Small wonder that the pastor is champing at the bit to resort to it. Yet it is also the least effective method of communication. So obviously he must learn to restrain himself in using it. Telling is used most frequently in intimate family circles—and again with great inefficiency. The mother complains about her daughter, "I keep telling her—but she doesn't listen!" By saying, "I keep telling her," she is insisting that she has done her part.

Yet the word *but* indicates that the two of them are playing a game which in Eric Berne's terminology could be called, IKTHB (*I Keep Telling Her, But*—). The daughter simply turns off her hearing aid when the telling begins. Through long association with the method, she has developed an automatic resistance to it. Rather than precipitating listening, *telling* blocks it. Actually the mother knows this, but she plays the game any-how. It has become a habit pattern from which she receives the satisfaction that she is doing her bit. She has the additional satisfaction of feeling sorry for herself when her daughter ignores her words. On the other hand, the daughter knows that her mother really doesn't expect her to listen, and so she feels safe in going her own way. At the same time she satisfies her need to rebel by defying her mother.

Telling is ineffective because it implies *telling off*. It has within it the barb of an attack which moves the hearer to erect his defenses. By presuming to know better, the teller places the hearer in a subordinate position. Unconsciously he may use the opportunity to tell as a justification for the release of his hostilities.

1. CONFRONTING vs. TELLING

Telling is not the only alternative to responding. In pastoral counseling there is also confrontation. Confrontation is less impulsive and more efficient than telling. Although confrontation is direct, it does not differ in spirit from responding.

Confrontation in counseling is made possible—and effective—by what Carl Rogers calls the three conditions in the counselor that make for a therapeutic experience. The first of these is a high degree of congruence—of genuineness. If the counseling is to be therapeutic the counselor's methods reflect his person rather than substitute for it. There is no professional facade, for in contrast to other professions, the counselor's person constitutes his profession.

The second condition is the counselor's care for the counselee as he is, without reservations or evaluations. Such care, however, is not without its pull to the future. The counselor respects the potentialities for growth and change. The genuineness of the counselor, then, is his honest-to-goodness concern for the counselee.

The third condition is his empathetic understanding. This understanding is from the inside—from a spirit-to-spirit identification. He accepts the private world of the counselee *as if* it were his own. The words *as if* are important because the private world of the counselee is not his own. His subjective involvement must remain in tension with his objective perspective. Otherwise his identification would reduce his empathy to impotence. While his one foot descends to the depths with the counselee, his other remains on *terra firma*. Thus each foot assists the other in performing the therapeutic task.

These three conditions help to bring about Rogers' fourth condition for a therapeutic experience, namely, a minimal perception of these qualities in the counselor by the counselee. If the congruence, care, and empathy are not perceived, their therapeutic predisposition is hindered. Confrontation may be the stimulus as well as the result of this perception. The counselor's qualities are sometimes demonstrated more forcefully by the obvious concern in confrontation than by the less obvious concern in responding. When the counselor confronts the counselee, he cares enough to risk offending him in order to help him. This could be the needed stimulus in opening the counselee's eyes and thus activating his potential to receive.

2. DIRECTNESS AND ANGER

The association of telling with telling-off extends also to confrontation. We tend to associate any directness with anger, perhaps because anger gives us the courage to be aggressive. What, then, would be the quality of such courage? Regardless of our answer, this is not an age in which to apologize for anger. In a day when disinterest and detachment are so widely adopted as defenses against becoming involved, the vitality and concern of anger are a wholesome relief. Rather than being passive and indifferent, the angry person is very involved, even though negatively. If he expresses his anger to the one with whom he is angry, he may shock him into his senses.

Because of this same sense of shock, however, his anger may also shut the door to further communication. The angry person is likely to say things more sharply than necessary and also to exaggerate. His courage is the momentary result of the triumph of his irritation over his fear. Anger integrates the person while fear disintegrates him. Nevertheless, anger itself often grows out of fear. The angry person may be hiding a frightened person.

The three friends of Job are cases in point. Job's calamity made them afraid. His expression of despair shook them to their foundations. Their angry reaction was in their own defense. Whatever fear they may have had of offending Job ("If one ventures a word with you, will you be offended?") was overcome by their greater indignation. They lost all reserve in their heated attempts to silence his threatening words. As often happens, they went too far in their anger, and the fierceness of their arguments brought at least a temporary halt to their relationship. Such violent exchanges have caused irreparable damage to many relationships, leaving not only permanent scars but unhealed wounds.

The difference between confrontation and telling-off begins in the motivation. Confrontation is less impulsive and more sensible. Impulsiveness goes with childlikeness. Anger is spontaneous rather than thought out. Children act out their feelings. They need parents to limit and direct them so that they learn as they grow up the discipline needed to reflect and evaluate in making decisions. The child's emotional impulsiveness in the meantime runs into conflict with parental suppression. Neither, however, is the end product in maturity.

Freud saw that the impulse-suppression conflict in the parent-child relationship continues throughout life. So he divided the person into an impulsive *id,* an opposing and suppressive super-ego, and an integrating ego to deal with the tension between them. If Freud believed that the superego was repressing the *id* and thereby causing neuroses, anti-Freudian psychologist O. Hobart Mowrer reminds us that releasing the *id* to dominate the superego may create only sociopaths.

Transactional analyst Eric Berne has chosen to keep the original historical context for the conflict and divides the person into a child, a parent, and an adult. We need all three, says Berne, but under varying circumstances. In other words, no one of these should be permanently recessive, but rather each should come forth when circumstances warrant it. The counselor is in a predominately adult role, and therefore the adult emphasis upon an intelligent grasp of the situation should predominate in determining when to confront. While the counselor may be motivated by irritation to confront, either from his impulsive child or his remonstrating parent, his confrontation most likely to stimulate the adult within the counselee is that motivated by his own adult. In this state he is free from the impulsiveness of the child and the suppressing influence of the parent to make a decision on the basis of intuitive and rational intelligence—an intelligence the Old Testament calls wisdom. "It is not the old that are wise, nor the aged that understand what is right," says Elihu, "but it is the spirit in a man that makes him understand." Such wisdom does not always imply premeditation. Spontaneous decisions may also be wise when their motivation is concern for another.

3. WITHIN EMPATHY AND RAPPORT

To confront a person is more than to present him with an insight. It is also to challenge him to face reality, to inspire him with expectations, to spur him into action. In line with the mutuality of the counseling relationship, the sharing of the counselee may stimulate the confronting by the counselor. Thus, confronting is not antithetical to responding but is in the same dynamic of involvement—perhaps even a further involvement. Confrontation takes place within the rapport of relationship and not apart from it. In fact it is the relationship itself that is often the decisive factor in the counselee's acceptance of the confrontation.

The difference in the effect on Job of Eliphaz and Elihu can be seen in this factor of relationship. In his first reaction to Job, Eliphaz offered a testimony to the faithfulness of God even in our sufferings. Yet Eliphaz' lack of response to Job's feelings prevented any rapport from developing, so that whatever good he may have offered was automatically resisted. He attempted to stifle Job's expression of despair by a ramming approach, and this is a far cry from confrontation.

Although he was equally convinced he had something to say, Elihu's confrontation said in effect, "I submit it to you for your response." "If you have anything to say, answer me; speak, for I desire to justify you." While the three friends made clear their intention to "shame" him for his "mocking," thus creating resistance rather than rapport, Elihu stimulated rapport by disavowing coercive tactics. "No fear of me need intimidate you," he said as he encouraged Job to speak his mind. This was a contrast to Zophar who said, "When you mock, shall no one shame you?" He intended to open all the stops in order to intimidate Job.

The directness of the three friends was a "hitting" directness. It expressed their reaction to Job—their defense against him. Elihu's directness was a confrontation because it was in the sharing rather than in the hitting dimension. It was, thus, a response to Job—an openness toward him. His rejection of Job's position and his presentation of alternate insights were offered within the empathy and rapport of a relationship, rather than in resistance to empathy and to the undermining of rapport. It is amazing how much a person can accept from a counselor when there is a relationship of empathy and rapport, and how little he will accept when this relationship is lacking.

Response and confrontation are part and parcel of the same empathetic concern. The one leads to the other in an interchangeable dynamic. There is no clash in gears when the pastor goes from responding to confronting. If there is, the confronting is coming from his child or his parent rather than from his adult. If our motivation is to help, whether we respond or confront, we are functioning within the same spirit or attitude. The connective is love—expressed in the wisdom of caring rather than in the mechanics of method.

Love is as aggressive as is anger in its caring, but it is positive rather than negative. Love, however, may include anger. The two are not always incompatible. The anger over injustice, both toward those who perpetrate it and those who permit it, may be an example of a love that cares. However, the anger of self-defense that comes into being when we are threatened is something other. Elihu admittedly was angry—at Job because he justified himself rather than God and at the three friends because they had no answer for Job even though they declared him to be in the wrong. Yet in his desire to assist Job and to be fair with him we sense in this anger also a love.

4. AGGRESSION IN THE FACE OF RESISTANCE

Confronting means presenting something to the counselee that he seemingly needs help in perceiving. It may be an insight into himself or his relationships that is slow in coming. It may be an alternative decision that the counselee seemingly has resistance to considering. It may be a suggestion that carries with it a touch of a shock because of the counselee's indisposition to hear it. It may be a challenge to act because the counselor senses the counselee is taking recourse in inaction. With his one foot at the level of the counselee's feelings he attempts to hoist him to the level of his other foot which is grounded on objective reality. The very fact that confronting may be necessary is an indication that it is not easy to do. Were there no resistance to it, the counselee would have in all probability become aware of what was needed on his own through his previous counseling. Since he has not, the counselor will need a backing of empathy to penerate the resistance.

Elihu perceived that Job was resistant to turning his head. He was looking at his calamity and listening for God's answer in only one direction. His arguments with the three friends had contributed to this fixed mind-set. Elihu desired to dislodge him from it so that he might have a more flexible view of things. This meant he would have to confront Job—but there had to be sufficient preparation for this. First he dissociated himself from the other three; then he created an acceptive atmosphere; next he restated how Job saw things as Elihu had understood him. Only after this prolonged buildup did he confront Job. "Behold, in this you are not right."

Yet he does more than simply voice his disagreement. "I will answer you." The confrontation continued as Elihu shared with Job what he felt was a wider vision. "Why do you say, 'He will answer none of my words?' For God speaks in one way and in two, though man does not perceive it." In other words, "Job, God may be speaking where you are not listening. Turn your head—for God speaks in more ways than your preconceived notions would indicate."

Confronting is harder for some pastors than for others. It requires the courage to risk offense, and some of us are so habituated to the need to please that we may unconsciously back away from introducing anything that might cause even temporary discomfort. We want nothing to endanger the counselee's mental image of us. To the degree that we are bound to this need to be approved—to be well liked—we may be blocked from offering the kind of help that is needed. The pastor who is Mr. Friendly may keep the atmosphere congenial, but he will not likely be a catalyst for growth.

Some pastors may seem more fitted to the listening function. They are passive in nature, and it is natural for them to let others talk and take the lead. To ask these "good listeners" to confront seems like asking them to change their personalities. Those who fall naturally into a listening position because of their passivity are rarely listeners to *feelings*. They listen in the sense of keeping the other person talking, but not in the sense of encouraging a therapeutic encounter. It requires a certain aggressiveness to respond to negative feelings like Job's despair—the same kind of aggressiveness that is needed to confront him with the inadequacy of his perspective.

Responding to feelings also requires courage. Responding, therefore, is really a form of confronting. The counselor is leading by following. Being selective in that to which he responds, he is in a sense directing the dialogue. The contrast, therefore, is not between leading and following but between confronting and evading. The counselor can evade by responding to the non-threatening aspects of the counselee's sharing and thereby distract the course of the conversation to more comfortable and superficial levels. The alternative is confrontation. He confronts either by responding to the feeling tone implied in the counselee's sharing, or he confronts by sharing with the counselee his own insights and concerns. "Behold, in this you are not right—I will answer you—God speaks in one way, and in two, though man does not perceive it."

A woman whom we can call Mrs. Jones had been sharing her marital problems with her pastor for four counseling sessions before she succeeded in bringing her husband along. During her previous counseling sessions, she had expressed her disappointment over her marriage because of her husband's irresponsible attitude. She also indicated suspicions concerning his fidelity.

When her husband accompanied her, the pastor received a different impression of Mrs. Jones than he had before. In his private sessions with her, he saw her as a very frustrated person who was at the end of her rope. With her husband he saw her as an officious mother-wife, who had brought her naughty boy to the pastor for his deserved rebuke. This threw considerable light on their difficulties. When he met with Mrs. Jones again, he was prepared to share this observation with her if she had not picked it up herself.

Mrs. J: Well, he came last time but he wouldn't come this time. I don't know what to do with him. I'm sorry he wasn't more cooperative. But that's the way he is! Now you know what I have to put up with. (She said this as though resigned to her lot.)

Pastor: How do you mean, that he wasn't cooperative?

Mrs. J: Well, you know—he just sat here and didn't contribute much.

I had to take the initiative like I always do. (This opened the door to the confrontation.)

Pastor: Yes, I noticed that. In fact I must admit it bothered me some. I don't know whether you were aware of it or not, but there were times when I would ask him something and you would answer.

Mrs. J: Oh, did I? Well he just sits there otherwise. (Obviously shook, but instinctively defensive.)

Pastor: Actually at these times I have in mind, you didn't give him a chance to answer.

Mrs. J: (Smiles weakly, trying to recover her poise.) Didn't I? I didn't realize.

Pastor: I didn't think you did, Mrs. Jones. Otherwise I am sure you wouldn't have done it. We can become so habituated to our way of doing things that we aren't aware of how it may seem to others. I'm just wondering whether Mr. Jones might not resent this type of taking over, regardless of how well-meaning you are.

Mrs. J: Well—maybe so. His mother is this way you know. She's a very domineering person—and Dick is just like a little boy when she's around. His father just stays out of her way.

Pastor: (He is aware of her attempt to shift the attention to his mother.) This is probably all the more reason why he would resent anything like this in you, isn't it? He's allergic to it— and, like his father, he is staying out of the way.

Mrs. J: (Looking struck.) I, ah, I see what you are driving at. Hm. But what am I going to do when he won't take hold? Just let things go to pot?

Pastor: At least it is a possible alternative to consider. As you have said, things are in a pretty sorry state—so maybe it wouldn't hurt to give it a try.

Mrs. J: I just don't know.

Pastor: You don't know whether you could?

Mrs. J: I was going to say—whether I *should*.

Pastor: It's a risk.

Mrs. J: Yes. (pause.)

Pastor: It wouldn't be easy. Habit patterns are hard to break.

Mrs. J: I want to think about this. I'm a little confused right now. I, ah, I just hadn't realized—I mean I just hadn't thought about this before. (pause.) My head's sort of swimming right now—I can't seem to concentrate.

The pastor realized that his confrontation had shaken Mrs. Jones, and he accepted her desire to let the matter rest for the time being. He hoped he had timed it wisely—that the preceding visits had created a sufficiently strong relationship to support this kind of directness. He also hoped that as a result of the confrontation Mrs. Jones herself would become more alert to her tendency to take over in the marriage.

When the pastor confronts in this manner he is not judging his counselee in the sense of rejecting her, although what he says may lead her to judge herself. Actually he is demonstrating his care for her. One of my students called regularly as a chaplain upon a patient in a mental hospital who was not much older than he. As he neared the end of the school year, the student was becoming discouraged with his progress. He had been responding to the best of his ability but to no perceptible avail. The patient was alert and affable, but he ran from any encounter with himself in terms of his failure to make an adult adjustment to life. Because of this, his prognosis was not hopeful.

On one of his last visits, as the patient again exhibited his characteristic evasiveness, the student spontaneously blurted out his concern. "Ben," he said, "it's just not good to run from these things. If you don't start coming to grips with yourself and your problems you may spend the rest of your life in an institution—and I don't want this to happen—not to you."

The patient stared at him for a moment and then said with similar spontaneity, "You care, don't you? You really care."

"Of course I care," said the student. "Didn't you know that?"

"No, not really," said the patient. "I'm sorry."

For the rest of the visit, they had a very meaningful conversation. I would like to think that the patient's somewhat unexpected improvement that followed was to some degree influenced by this breakthrough of concern—and its perception. The student's concerned confrontation had done what his reponding had not done. It had penetrated the defenses of one who felt no one cared beyond his professional duty.

The perception of this concern is at the basis of our healing ministry. After I had called repeatedly upon a sick parishioner, her husband thanked me with so much feeling that I felt constrained to pass it off. "I'm just doing my duty," I said. His face dropped. "I don't really believe that, pastor," he said. "At least I'd rather not."

Elihu's concern is really not mitigated by his honest confession, "I must speak, that I may find relief." Nor does it detract from the wisdom of what he had to offer.

"Because of the multitude of oppressions people cry out; they call for help because of the arm of the mighty. But none says, 'Where is God my Maker, who gives songs in the night?' "

XI

THE EXPERIENCE OF KNOWING

Job 38–42

1. OUT OF THE WHIRLWIND GOD SPEAKS

"Then the Lord answered Job out of the whirlwind." The Elihu transition was over, and the encounter with God had begun. The significance of the word *whirlwind* is open to conjecture. Storms often accompany revelatory experiences in the Old Testament. Certainly the effect on Job was like a storm, and the whirlwind could be descriptive of his inner experience.

While Job was on the receiving end of the theophany, he was anything but uninvolved. Like the experience of the apostle Paul when he was caught up to the third heaven, Job probably would find it difficult to describe in words what happened. Yet its effect on him was sufficient to change his whole way of looking at things. It was an experience in *knowing* out of which the understanding Job so earnestly wanted would come—and it would be his *own*.

Is Elihu still speaking in the whirlwind? There is no mention of his words being ended as is usual in the dialogue. The course that Elihu was taking at the close of his involvement—beholding

God's mighty acts in creation—was the same course that God took throughout the theophany. For Job, God is speaking. Whether he is speaking through Elihu or not would be immaterial. The means become unimportant when one hears God speaking to him.

Nevertheless the lack of any line of demarcation between Elihu's ministry and Job's encounter in the whirlwind is in the nature of good pastoral care. The pastor is the mediator or midwife to the counselee's own involvement with God, and when this involvement takes place, he fades out of the picture. This transfer from pastor to God is inherent in the approach and spirit of pastoral care as we have observed it in Elihu. The head of the church is known through the members of his Body. Within the human ministry the dialogue with God takes place. Good pastoral care like good preaching leads people to their own encounter with God and does not try to *be* the encounter.

Job wanted his encounter with God so that he could question God, but when the encounter actually came, it was God who questioned Job. "Who is this that darkens counsel [denies providence] by words without knowledge? Gird up your loins like a man, I will question you, and you shall declare to me." Job's encounter had come, but it was God who presented the agenda and not Job. "Where were you when I laid the foundation of the earth?" So began the questions regarding God's creative wonders that Elihu had initiated. "Can you, like him, spread out the skies, hard as a molten mirror?"

The questions raised by Elihu and by God are still valid in spite of the fact that over two thousand years have passed with a phenomenal increase in scientific understanding. Though we can better describe these natural phenomena, we still cannot duplicate them. We are yet confronted by mystery. The more we know scientifically, the more we realize we do not yet know—and the more we marvel at nature. The paradox is illustrated by the scientist who was asked to respond by telegram in one hundred words concerning his research findings into a certain phenomenon. He spelled out the words "don't know" fifty times.

Inquiries into the foundations of the earth and of the sea are, if anything, more fascinating today than ever. The potentialities of the sea are intriguing as we think ahead concerning how the world of science may exploit them for human benefit. While we would conceptualize the foundations of the earth differently than the ancient poet, we also like to speculate about the composition of the inside of the earth. Day and night are still our basis for the measurement of time, and while we understand more about the special forces and rotations of the sun and the earth, we are no less dependent upon them. The rain and hail and snow are exasperating when they frustrate our plans. We are still helpless for the most part when it comes to controlling the weather. If the poet could have looked into the snow crystals through a microscope, what would he have said about the myriad of designs, intricate and symmetrical! And the stars! Although astrology has given way scientifically to astronomy, our heads swim even more because of our greater understanding of the stratosphere. The very distances involved in the concept of light years leaves us lost in our ability to comprehend.

While civilization is fast doing away with the animals which God mentions, the lion, the mountain goat, the wild ass, the ostrich, the hawk, and the horse, each is as much an object of marvel as ever. The majesty of the lion, the surefootedness of the goat, the soaring of the hawk are still fascinating to the poet, the artist, and the zoologist. In spite of how little they affect our lives except as curiosity pieces in the zoo, we are reluctant to have them become extinct. Sentimentally we count the few remaining whooping cranes and feel better when their diminishing numbers hold their own. The speed of the cheetah is amazing even in an age of speed cars. The intelligence of the dolphin is creating much contemporary interest. The strength of the horse is a unit in the measurement of power. "Do you give the horse his might? . . . Is it by your wisdom that the hawk . . . spreads his wings toward the south?"

2. NOT ETHICS BUT POWER

There is no ethical content to God's revelation, only a stress on his majesty, power, and genius. He makes no attempt morally to justify his ways with Job or to acknowledge the existence of any moral demand. This is the point that Jung makes in his *Answer to Job*. It is Job who raises the ethical questions while God answers only with intimidation. Job expresses the cry of outrage from moral man at the arbitrariness of the deity. "I was at ease and he broke me asunder . . . although there was no violence in my hands and my prayer is pure." Charging God directly he asks, "Does it seem good to thee to oppress, to despise the work of thy hands and favor the designs of the wicked?"

Yet who can argue with God? The moral protest is crushed by the heavy hand of the deity. "What he desires, that he does." Who can call him to account? "When I consider, I am in dread of him." The image of God in man does not seem to correspond to God's real essence. The creature is more ethical than the Creator. When the Creator gets caught in man's ethical squeeze, as he did with Job, he reacts by flexing his muscles to divert attention from the moral indefensibility of his actions. Job's three friends tried to take God off the hook, but Job was determined that they should not succeed. Yet Job himself is ambivalent toward God. After charging the three friends with being partial to

143

God, he went on to warn them that such partiality was displeasing to *God*. In refusing to weaken before the pressure of the three, he swore to his innocence by the same God whom he accused of wronging him.

As Elihu had predicted, Job was overwhelmed by this demonstration of God's power. He was humbled into submission, beaten down rather than convinced. When God said, "He who argues with God, let him answer it," Job answered the Lord, "Behold, I am of small account; what shall I answer thee? I lay my hand on my mouth. I have spoken once, and I will not answer; twice, but I will proceed no further." I have already put my foot in my mouth, and from now on I am keeping it shut. That which Job had asked not to happen was now happening. The dread of God was terrifying him. When God calls, how then can he answer? He is overpowered by the *mysterium tremendum*. Elihu's warning is fulfilled, "Shall it be told him that I would speak? Did a man ever wish that he would be swallowed up?" Silenced by humiliation Job sees, but not really. Like the blind man upon whose eyes Jesus put clay and told him to wash, he sees "trees as men walking." Another application of clay was needed before he would see clearly. So God continued with the same approach from nature as before.

Again God told Job to gird up his loins for questioning. "Will you put me in the wrong?" he asks. "Will you condemn me that you may be justified? Have you an arm like God?" Does God owe Job anything? Has he even a moral responsibility to Job? Can God be called to account by man? Again the ethical issue is bypassed in favor of the argument from power. "Behold the hippopotamus, which I made as I made you." Who has not been intrigued by this monster with the huge mouth? "Can you draw out the crocodile with a fishhook?" What could be worse than to be thrown to the crocodiles?

If God's purpose was to humble Job, why keep on with this line of argument? Could God have something else in mind? If he did, Job's second opportunity to speak showed the difference. Though there is nothing ethical in God's approach, it produced an ethical result. Job repented in dust and ashes. "I know that thou canst do all things, and that no purpose of thine can be thwarted. 'Who is this that hides counsel without knowledge?' Therefore I have uttered what I did not understand, things too wonderful for me which I did not know."

3. THE CHANGE IN JOB

What got through on the repetition of the same application was that God cared. His persistence revealed to Job his concern behind his power. Through this involvement with God in terms of the marvels of creation, Job began to hear—to see—the gospel of his love. Job's response demonstrates the relationship between being cared for and being able to look at oneself. God's love is not called forth by its object, for it is its own stimulus. Therefore, there is no pressure upon the object—in this case, Job—to justify himself. The basis for pastoral care is in its demonstration of this divine acceptance—in its involvement in the good news that God cares. It is this gospel rather than the law (the thou shalts and thou shalt nots) that produces ethical commitment. Yet like Eliphaz, Bildad, and Zophar, we still seem to labor under the impression that the law produces repentance, that morality comes out of moralizing, and that change in character comes through threats of consequential punishment.

God answered none of Job's questions. In fact he indicated that they were the wrong questions, based upon erroneous and even presumptuous preconceptions. Instead, he involved Job in the experience of knowing him through his creative activity. Job's

145

questions about the ways of God could not be answered apart from this knowing of God himself. Through the experience of *knowing*, Job's entire perspective changed. The same is true also in human relationships. The impressions one may have of another from observing him or hearing about him, may change completely after he gets to know him. To attempt to understand a person's behavior apart from knowing him is to ignore the difference between a person and a thing—an *it* and a *thou*.

Psychiatrist Viktor Frankl is fond of quoting Nietzsche's saying, "He who knows the *why* can bear with any *how*." Out of this conviction Frankl has developed his logotherapy which places the need for meaning—the *logos*—as the fundamental human need. Job takes us beyond Frankl. During his dialogues with the three friends, he also expressed the conviction that if he knew the *why* of his calamities, he could endure them. "I will say to God . . . let me know why thou dost contend against me." Consequently he desired an encounter with God. At times he even believed he could convince God by his arguments. "Behold, I have prepared my case; I know that I shall be vindicated." At other times he felt he had no chance with God. "God has made my heart faint; the Almighty has terrified me; for I am hemmed in by darkness, and thick darkness covers my face."

After his encounter Job still does not know the *why*. Yet he seems to accept the *how*. The reason—he knows the *Who*. He who knows the *Who*, therefore, can bear with any *how* even though he knows not the *why*. Knowing the *Who* without knowing the *why* leaves room for faith. It brings security without having answers. The experience of love makes pressing questions less pressing.

The change in Job that resulted from his religious experience took place before any restoral or even hope for restoral of his former possessions. It was a change from within that in turn affected the way he looked at life. Job had had his encounter, and the experience of knowing what came from it gave to his reason the support it needed to make sense out of life. His perception of *meaning* at this point was intuitive rather than rational. Out of the revelation of God's majesty, power, and wisdom finally came the revelation of his providential care—his love.

The word *love* is not mentioned, but the account that Job gave of his new relationship with God is descriptive of the security of love. Repentance is an experience that follows the realization of grace. Job had a change of heart that brought not only a realistic look at himself but also a realistic hope. Since God made it clear that he owed Job nothing, his hope was obviously based on grace. Job was humbled but no longer humiliated. He felt secure in his new knowledge of God. "Hear and I will speak." Although in the theophany it was God who did the asking, Job now feels free enough in the relationship to take the initiative. "I will question you and you declare to me." The quest for answers goes on, but no longer out of the anguish of alienation.

Job described his change as one of *seeing* rather than *hearing*. "I had heard of thee by the hearing of the ear, but now my eye sees thee." Elihu had informed Job that God speaks in one way and in two, though man does not perceive it. Now Job perceives it. His eyes are open. The contrast between the hearing of the ear and the seeing of the eye points to sight as the clearer sense of perception.

Although seeing is a figurative expression for the perception of the soul, there is a parallel in the medium of the Sacrament in Christian worship. Job's seeing was also sacramental in nature since God utilized his mask, the world of creation, to reveal himself. That no man shall see God and live is a familiar biblical theme. The "naked God" is too much for us. As creatures in a sensory habitat, we are dependent upon the medium of the tangible for our perception of the intangible. In such perception, *seeing* is the sense that communicates most fully. Job's experience is comparable to that of Isaiah who saw God in a vision, "sitting upon a throne, high and lifted up." The spiritual integration that followed this experience of seeing is also similar. Isaiah said, "Woe is me! For I am lost; for I am a man of unclean lips." Job said, "I despise myself, and repent in dust and ashes."

These words of Job were precisely what the three friends had been pressing him to say. Yet in the way they went about it they only pushed him further from saying them. Now Job says them voluntarily—even spontaneously—out of his own conviction. Ironically, however, Job's "arrival" is no triumph for the three friends. In the epilogue God directed Job to offer sacrifice and to intercede for them, saying that he would accept Job's prayer "not to deal with them according to their folly." We are loved into repentance and not clubbed into it.

Job now sees the righteousness which he defended before the attacks of the three friends as "filthy rags." His previous attitude and rash statements toward God he views as arrogant ignorance. "I have uttered what I did not understand." He regrets saying what he did, for he no longer sees things in the same light. He is looking at his same problems but from a different perspective. Hence he repents concerning his total self—his whole behavior. Courageously even though naïvely he had exposed himself in his despair to judgment. Now he has experienced this judgment as a self-judgment. He also experienced God's acceptance in spite of it. Perhaps this was why he could judge himself. The new look at God that had come from his experience of knowing had given him a new look at himself and a new look at his fellows. His despair had been converted into repentance, and now he could sorrow with hope.

As a result of his change, Job's attitude in questioning God is also different. He is open now to receive. Before, his questioning was actually protesting. His *why* was a cry of outrage. "Behold I cry out 'Violence!' but I am not answered." His protest has been resolved in the subsequent experience of knowing. Now his questions are really questions.

O. Hobart Mowrer might say that Job's guilt was real and therefore could not be resolved until his confession was followed by works of atonement. Job's guilt was real—no doubt about this. He put it in the strongest of words, "I despise myself." But Mowrer not withstanding, forgiveness is also real. Not all grace is cheap. There is also real grace. Real forgiveness is unconditional forgiveness. The sinner is accepted as he is. In Elihu's words, the mediator is gracious to the sinner and delivers him, having found a ransom. If there is no real forgiveness, there is also no real love. Then there would be no real hope, only despair. But instead, Job repents. He had hope. In knowing God he knew the forgiveness of God.

Yet there is an ethical response. In the epilogue Job interceded for his offending friends. This is a response to his own forgiveness. But it is a response that came after his sins were forgiven and not as an atonement in response to his guilt. In the biblical perspective motives are taken into account as well as actions. If our ethical conduct is an atonement to quiet the discomfiture of guilt, it stems from something less than self-giving love. The ability to love comes from the experience of being loved. So the ability to forgive and to intercede comes from the experience of being forgiven.

4. WHAT JOB RECEIVED

The sequence in the movement of Job's religious crisis began with his calamities which brought about his depression and subsequent catharsis. When his catharsis was resisted by his three counselors, Job reacted in defiance and became defensive to the point of shutting off all communications. Through Elihu's empathetic identification his defenses were lowered and he experienced a relationship of rapport. Through this medium Elihu confronted him with a widening vision of God's ways. Then came his religious experience. Though humbled at first, Job was led by the theophany to know God in his forgiving love. He repented. In so doing he died to the old man and was resurrected to the new man. While yet in despair Job had surges of hope that God would vindicate him. Now that God had spoken, Job had his vindication. All things had become new because he himself had become new. Our language is New Testament-like in its imagery. Therefore, we could with some justification conclude with Paul's words, "All this is from God who through Christ reconciled us to himself."

The epilogue poses a problem. After Job's experience of *knowing* in which he found his answer in the midst of his troubles, the restoration of his blessings seems anticlimactic. Regardless of what we may think of the epilogue and its place in the book, the restoration of Job's losses is symbolic of the resurrection of Job himself.

Since Job had his experience of knowing before the restoration of his possessions, what was it that he really had received? He had *God*. If he had answers, Eliphaz' position would have prevailed. The only difference between them, then, would be that Job had better answers—a difference in degree rather than in kind. Yet the answer is not in *answers* but in an experience of knowing. The difference is a difference in kind. When Elihu stood with Job to look with marvel at God's creative genius, he was recognizing mystery rather than providing answers.

Job's religious experience is marked by mystery. Not only is mystery implied by the image of the whirlwind, but it is involved in the encounter itself and also in its outcome. The very presence of God means mystery. To try and eliminate it as Eliphaz did by feeling compelled to supply answers, is in reality an attempt to bypass God. To let God be God is to accept the presence of mystery. It is to let our faith in God stand in spite of our lack of understanding. Actually it is an acceptance by the counselor of his own finitude—of his own creatureliness.

Job had "songs in the night." Elihu's insight was realized. While the masses of men cry out for help in their troubles because of the arm of the mighty, none by contrast has the spiritual maturity to say, "Where is God my Maker, who gives songs in the night?" Perhaps it was this confrontation by Elihu that prepared the way for Job to know its meaning. In the midst of his troubles rather than through their removal, Job triumphed over his despair. Because he knew the One in whom he believed, his spirit had become positive.

The Book of Job is not only a drama of a man's trust in God, but also a drama of God's trust in a man. The critical issue is whether Job feared God for nought. After his ordeal Job was different. He could not have remained the same. He was shaken to his foundations. The faith that preceded the ordeal was not the faith that brought him "songs in the night." Before, the question, "Does Job fear God for nought?" seemed not to have entered Job's mind. In those days of prosperity he thought, "I shall die in my nest, and I shall multiply my days as the sand." During his ordeal, however, this question became the major issue. "What advantage have I? How am I better off than if I had sinned?" The question was too threatening for the three friends, and they evaded it. Elihu had the courage not only to restate it but to talk directly to it. As a result of his ordeal Job at least knew what the question meant.

If Job were to reflect upon his experience, what would he say that could be passed on to a kindred sufferer? He was a counselor himself before his ordeal. "Men listened to me, and waited, and kept silence for my counsel." He implied to the three friends that his counseling had been like theirs. "I also could speak as you do, if you were in my place." But now, after the ordeal, how would he change his approach?

While admittedly in the realm of conjecture, I would imagine Job saying that no answers can be given to the sufferer apart from the struggle in the sufferer's own soul. It is the struggle itself that leads to the experience of knowing. Whatever answers are pertinent to the sufferer come through his own involvement in the *knowing* process. The pastoral counselor is a support in the struggle to bring to birth, though by labor and travail. To attempt to spare the sufferer the ordeal of his own struggle with God is to disrespect his individuality as a person. It is one thing to hear of God by the hearing of the ear; it is another to see him with one's own eyes. Only then can he *know*.

INDEX